LIFE CYCLE OF BIRDS

(A Pictorial Presentation)

Text & Photographs

Bhagat Singh

F-2/16, Ansari Road, Daryaganj, New Delhi-110002
☎ 23275434, 23262683, 23262783 • Fax: 011-23257790
E-mail: info@unicornbooks.in • *Website:* www.unicornbooks.in

Publisher : **UNICORN BOOKS**
ISBN : 978-81-7806-203-7

FOREWORD

Birds have always fascinated humankind and bird-watching or birding has become hugely popular all over the world. Among all the life forms on Earth, birds are certainly the most admired, most studied and most defended and can be found virtually everywhere throughout the world.

The association between human beings and birds has been long and intimate. In fact, birds have helped humankind in various ways—from the geese whose warning cries saved Rome to the canaries that were used to warn coal miners of methane gas leakage. Birds continue to provide lifesaving service by acting as reliable indicators of the health of our environment, especially regarding the dangers arising from chemicals and other toxic substances in the atmosphere. Moreover, birds play a vital role in maintaining the balance of nature by controlling insect pests and rodents as well as in cross-pollination of plant species, in seed dispersal and as scavengers. Further, there are birds that have made remarkable contributions to human welfare, economically and otherwise. The classic case is that of India's wonder bird, the Red Junglefowl, which is the progenitor of all poultry forms worldwide and has been valuable in contributing to medical research and human health. No wonder it has been said that birds can exist without humankind, but humankind cannot exist without birds.

Most people enjoy bird-watching for fun and as pastime. This joy can be greatly enhanced by an understanding of the lifecycle of different bird species. This book by Shri Bhagat Singh is aimed precisely in this direction and will surely generate greater awareness and appreciation of the various aspects of birdlife as well as hopefully contribute to safeguarding and improving the lives of the wonderful winged creatures that play such a valuable role in nature and for the benefit of humankind.

This pictorial publication has certain special features that need mention. First, it covers several different bird species found in India, many of which are quite common and yet information on their lifecycles are not readily available in the manner given in this book. The introductory part of the book provides very useful notes on various aspects of birdlife, more specially on lifecycle issues. Then, the book includes species-wise accounts on selected bird species that are insightful and equally informative. All this will surely be found useful by the lay bird lover as well as those more seriously interested in the subject.

The second special feature of the book is clearly the pictorial part, with several outstanding true-to-life photographs of different bird species in their natural settings. Each photograph is clear, sharp and stunning. These pictures greatly enhance the value of the book and make it distinctive indeed. In this sense, perhaps this is the only publication of its type to date.

It is further noteworthy that all the photographs in the book have been taken by the author himself. This is testimony of his passionate and abiding interest in the subject and his deep understanding of the same. It is also indicative of his extraordinary perseverance and patience as well as his exceptional photographic skills honed over the years. Here, it is necessary to add that Shri Bhagat Singh has been a lover of nature and especially birds for over four decades. He has been observing, studying and photographing birds over the years with a passion that is simply amazing and rare. In recent years, he has authored two separate books on the birds of Uttarakhand and Rajasthan. It is wonderful that this time he is contributing this delightful volume on the lifecycle of birds, which will surely be found useful by all concerned.

I have had the good fortune of knowing Shri Bhagat Singh for some years and have had the benefit of receiving some of his deep knowledge on birds and also his amazing photographs. I have admiration for his scholarship, his zeal for and advocacy of nature conservation and his highly genial and affable temperament.

SAMAR SINGH
Former Secretary to the Government of India, Secretary General WWF-India & President, WPA-India.

MAN AND BIRD

The "World of Birds" is the most beautiful and colourful gift of nature to mankind. Their brilliant colours, innumerable forms, gorgeous flights, playful acts, full of fun and frolic, and melodies greeting the new-born dawn bestow upon these magnificent denizens of the sky a place of honour and pride among the comity of living on our planet. Since time immemorial, birds have had a close relationship with human population. The whistling tunes of Thrush, sonnets of Bulbul, mournful lament of Hoopoe, hooting of Owl, out-cry of Red Jungle Fowl, chattering of Myna, drum-beats of Barbet, ascending notes of Koel, emotional outburst of Chatak, distressed cry of Chakor, maddening call-notes of Papiya, melodies of Shyama, piercing scream of Peacock, ornamental dance of Saras, soft touch of Kapot (Pigeon), fluting tunes of Robin, lyrics of Madhuka (lora), rhythmic walk of Hans (Swan), and a great variety of fun-filled and joyous acts of a large multitude of birds have aroused emotions and passions in human hearts and influenced human folklore and literature.

Let us all express our heartfelt gratitude to these winged angels of the sky. Let us also resolve that from hereon, we will treat these winged creatures with love, affection and respect, that they so truly deserve.

Monal Pheasant

CONTENTS

PREFACE

Birds are the most lustrous ornaments of our forests. They are sparkling jewels that float over our lakes, rivers and water courses. They adorn our homes, beautify our gardens, and entertain us with their sweet melodies and gorgeous flights.

Conservation of birds is a matter of great concern for all. Each one of us owns the responsibility to preserve and protect the miracles of birdlife that thrives today. We can do this by knowing as much about these winged creatures as we can. The present book has been designed to cater to the needs of all, who are concerned with the future of birdlife, and the unspoilt beauty of our land. I hope it will find many appreciative readers, who care for the beauty and variety of birds, and will cooperate honestly in the endeavour to protect this natural heritage, the Mother Nature has preserved for ages for all of us. This book provides true insight into the various phases of growth of the birdlife through true-to-life photographs, and meets the long desired need of nature lovers and amateur birdwatchers alike.

Endeavour of this kind requires inspiration, psychological support, reassurance and the love of some dear ones. My little grand-daughters – Ayushi and Anjali – gave me all this in full measure. I am also thankful to Aman Sood, a dedicated young birdwatcher, who enthusiastically accompanied me on several of my field excursions, and helped me in locating nests in dense forests, and making arrangements, with remarkable skill, for safe access to them, to enable me to take close-up shots of the eggs and the nestlings, taking due care that no damage is done to the nest and no disturbance is caused to the breeding birds. The much needed support of this kind strengthened my determination to accomplish the formidable task of presenting to the people at large, and to birdwatchers and nature lovers in particular, the miracles of birdlife in its various phases of growth through colourful photographs. I trust they will find time to explore the rich bird wealth of our country and contribute their bit to the effort to preserve and protect, whatever now remains of it, to ensure that there are birds for the future generations to see and enjoy.

Copper smith

INTRODUCTION

Over 8500 species of birds are known in the world today. In most of the countries, people are interested in birds to a greater or lesser degree. Apart from scientific studies undertaken by ornithologists in evolution and general biology of birds, the amateur bird-watchers have made important contribution to our knowledge of birdlife. It is not necessary to make scientific observations to be a bird watcher. Bird watching is a good sport. Majority of bird watchers watch birds just because they derive incalculable mental refreshment and joy from this simple pastime.

People, nowadays, are becoming more and more conscious that they can not live a healthy life, independent of their natural environment. Birds, in this context, perform an invaluable function. They warn us, by their health and well-being, of the dangers that threaten us in the environment. Several species of birds have become extinct or miserably dwindled in numbers, as a result of pesticide residues in the environment. This warns us that we too are absorbing all kinds of chemicals into our own bodies, which have unpredictable side effects, fraught with dire consequences to our healthy growth. This warns us that this is high time that we must take effective and concrete action to stop all toxic substances getting into the environment. If we are able to put a halt to this terrible decline, we will have the satisfaction that we are helping ourselves as well as these magnificent winged creatures.

Birds have a remarkable range of behaviour. Many of their habits are exceedingly intricate. For example, nest-building in some species involves a wide range of activities including the choice of a proper site, selection of right materials – often different at different stages in the building operations – and a number of weaving and turning movements. Even young birds breeding for the first time may successfully undertake these activities, and go on to raise a family.

Though much still remains a mystery, we now know a great deal more about the behaviour of birds. A number of behaviour patterns are innate in that the bird is born with the ability to do them. Many of the bird's activities are learned and perfected during its life. Certain aspects of songs of many birds are inherited. However, all the inherited activities are not perfect, and the bird has to use them time and again in order to master them. Contact with others of its own species certainly helps the bird to perfect them. Hence, many activities may include innate aspects as well as those perfected by practice and copied from other individuals. Watching others of its own species and copying their behaviour is an obvious way in which young birds can learn to cope with their environment. It is very important that young birds learn as quickly as possible which objects are dangerous and which pose no threat. For many species, particularly for smaller ones, the early days after leaving the nest are very important, and the parent's guidance extremely valuable. Nevertheless, the young birds survive sufficiently well for the species to prosper.

Learning by trial and error and continued practice is also very important. Birds have evolved their complex range of habits in relation to what has proved best for them in their natural surroundings.

Passerines, by and large, produce songs prior to breeding season (Little Pied Flycatcher)

Songs: Birds produce songs mainly during periods prior to breeding, when territories are being set up and courtship undertaken. Bird songs are highly characteristic, each species usually having a very distinct song. By singing, a male bird announces his claim to a territory and also endeavours to attract a mate. By and large, song is produced by the males, and not by females of a species.

Blue-headed Rockthrush giving mating call during breeding period

Warning and Fear: In a number of circumstances, birds give calls to draw the attention of other birds towards an approaching predator so as to enable it to take evasive action. For the vast majority of birds, there is always the threat of danger lurking somewhere. In such a situation, discretion is the better part of valour. Once an enemy is identified, the bird can take appropriate action. If the predator is a mammal, the bird can easily avoid it by staying clear of the ground. If, however, the threat comes from another bird, then it must be avoided in another way. This might entail diving into thick bushes, on to or under water, or trying to outpace it, depending on the species of bird threatened, and the area in which it is. Often such flight is accompanied by alarm calls, warning the neighbouring birds of the threat. Parent birds give alarm calls in order to protect their offspring, and secondly there are occasions when there is safety in numbers, by grouping tightly together the birds may be able to make it difficult for the attacking predator to single out and catch any one individual.

Young birds generally learn to recognize many of their enemies from the reactions of their parents. They also learn to recognize and give the calls. Small birds, still in the nest, will crouch and remain silent, when they hear their parents warn of an approaching predator. They learn to do this before they are a week old.

Birds give alarm calls to draw attention of other birds towards an approaching predator (Indian Roller)

Young birds, still in nest, crouch and remain silent, when their parents warn of an approaching predator (Yellow-eyed Babbler – Nestlings)

Feeding: For lack of teeth, birds do not chew their food at all. Majority of birds eat their prey whole. Many birds such as Warblers, Thrushes, Finches etc. generally take prey of smaller size, which could be swallowed. Some birds like Ducks and game birds may eat foliage.

Feeding, sometimes, becomes dangerous for the birds. While feeding, they run the risk of not noticing the approach of a predator until it is too late. Drinking too is often dangerous. Some birds obtain most of their water from their food, especially the insectivores and the birds of prey, which may hardly need to drink. But other birds need water to drink. In doing so, they expose themselves to predators. This is specially true in drier regions, where birds congregate in large numbers at water holes, which become favourite hunting grounds for birds of prey.

Some species include fruits in their diet
(Green Barbet on Amla tree)

Seeds: A wide variety of birds eat seeds of plants. Amongst the non-passerines, Pigeons, Parakeets and Woodpeckers are the prominent ones. Among the passerines, Tits, Nuthatches and Finches are seed eaters. The bills of these species are specially adapted to deal with seeds, which are generally hard structures, and are difficult to eat. A few of the seed-eating species eat seeds the whole year round. Tits are largely insectivorous during the summer months. Many of the Finches feed their young both insects and seeds. The reason for feeding insects to the young is perhaps

Flowers become source of food for birds, particularly in temperate forests, when, due to rigours of climate, they face acute scarcity of insect-food

Rufous-breasted Pied Woodpecker climbing up the tree-trunk in search of insects behind the bark

that insects are richer in proteins than the seeds are. Secondly, insect food contains large quantities of water, which is necessary for the healthy growth of young birds. Some smaller birds such as Tits and Nuthatches store seeds in crevices in the bark from which they retrieve them later.

Fruits: Fruits are often relatively large in size and, as a result, many of the fruit-eating species have evolved wide bills and gapes, enabling them to swallow the fruits whole. Once swallowed, the soft fruits are easily digested. Fruits are highly digestible, and seeds are not, and so usually pass through the gut undamaged. Birds that eat fruits distribute and spread around seeds, and thus, help in the evolution of fruiting plants.

Insects: Besides small passerine insectivores, a great variety of birds eat insects. Many of these such as Warblers, which have small all-purpose bills, look unspecialized for this purpose. The reasons for this are that many insectivorous species turn to other foods at other times of the year. Some birds such as Tits and Warblers eat fruits but they can not be, for obvious reasons, full-time insectivore in temperate regions.

The truly specialized insectivores which live on insects the whole year round, may, broadly, be divided into two categories; (i) the birds, which have stubby bills and huge gapes; and (ii) the birds having long pointed bills. The birds with long pointed bills such as Bee-eaters catch flying insects, and then return to a perch, where they set down to eat their prey.

The birds that have stubby bills and broad gapes, such as Nightjars, take large insects. Some birds such as Swifts and Swallows take smaller prey. The birds which feed on aerial insects are, to a great extent, dependent on good supplies the year round. They generally do not change their diet. But most of the birds, that seek their prey in temperate areas, move to spend the winter in tropical climate.

Many species of birds, such as Swallows, Bee-eaters and Flycatchers, hawk insects on the wing; whereas Warblers glean insects from the foliage. Tree-creepers and Nuthatches climb up and down the trunk of trees searching for insects hidden behind the bark. The most specialized birds that take insects from the trunks of trees are the Woodpeckers, which drill holes into the burrows of beetle larvae and take out the grubs with their long tongues. The tip of the tongue of these birds is generally barbed or sticky enabling them to grip their prey.

Many large birds feed on large prey (Serpent Eagle)

Collared Blackbird digging soft earth for insects

Many large birds, such as Rollers, Hoopoes and Hornbills, feed on large insects. Birds of prey too may take insects. Some Falcons and Black kites include a high proportion of insects in their diet.

Omnivores: Many species of birds include a great variety of food in their diet. Some have seasonal variation in their diet; while there are many that take a wide range of food at all the times of the year. The common Starling is an example of such a species. They may live in rural or urban areas; feed on worms in the meadows;

and may move to the woods at the end of the nesting season, along with their young to reap the caterpillars. Soon after, they may return to gardens to feed on early soft fruits. Other scavengers such as Kites are good at eating anything available from rubbish dumps to dead animals. All these birds could be called omnivores.

There are a number of species that specialize on feeding of nectar. Amongst them, the most striking are tiny brilliantly coloured Hummingbirds, which possess wonderful skill to take nectar from flowers. There are also Sunbirds, which are small but are often brightly coloured. They too hover at flowers to obtain nectar. The White-eyes can roll the tongue into a tube, and suck the nectar into their mouths.

Sunbird sucking nectar from flowers

Birds, that are wholly dependent on a special diet, may face inherent dangers. If the diet becomes scare or disappears, their very existence is threatened. In such circumstances, some birds, such as Whitebreasted Kingfishers, adapt themselves to take to new form of food, different from their traditional diet.

Some birds adapt to new form of diet, when their traditional food disappears or becomes scarce (White-breasted Kingfisher)

HABITATS

Temperate Forests: Temperate forests could broadly be divided into coniferous and broad-leaved woodlands. Food supply in these forests varies markedly with the seasons. This has overwhelming effects on birdlife in them. The trees put on new growth in spring and produce fruits in autumn. Insect larvae, it is well-known, grow best on tender leaves. In summer, winged insects are more abundant. However, both of these become scarce as early winter frosts occur. The insect eating birds have either to change their diet or move down to warmer areas at lower elevations.

Many birds such as Tits, Jays and Nuthatches store seeds in large quantities, and use them during hard winter, when days are short, and searching times reduced.

Woodpeckers are characteristic birds of temperate woodlands. They mostly extract beetle larvae from dead or damaged timber with their long tongues, which have barbed or sticky tips. Many of them also eat seeds, if the need be.

Holes in trees provide nesting sites for a wide variety of birds. These nests are relatively safe from predators such as large birds and most ground mammals. Woodpeckers, Owls, Tits, Redstarts, Nuthatches, some

Temperate forest with mixed growth of a wide variety of trees and undergrowth are favourite hunting ground for many species of birds, such as Woodpeckers, Finches, Tits, Babblers, Laughing Thrushes, etc.

Upper Temperate forests with dwarf trees, interspersed with scattered rocky meadows provide habitat and food to high-altitude birds, particularly in winter

Flycatchers and Warblers nest in holes in trees. These birds raise large broods than those nest in exposed sites. Large broods need more quantities of food. Hence, parent birds require longer period to raise the young than those which are reared in open cup-shaped nests.

The wide range of animal life in temperate forests has resulted in a number of predatory birds. The Sparrow-Hawks, for example, are specialists at catching birds by chasing them among the branches. Many Owls, that live in temperate forests, kill both small birds and mammals by hunting in the dark. They locate their prey by sound.

Sub-Tropical Forests: Sub-tropical forests provide richest and most exciting habitats to the animal and plant life. The towering trees and the stillness inside the forest have a quality of their own. The warmth of these forests makes relatively small demands on warm-blooded creatures.

The trees in sub-tropical areas usually remain green for most part of the year, but some species shed all their leaves and remain leafless for a short period. The trees are often very tall with closed canopy on the top. Little light reaches the forest floor, and only small shrubs and saplings of large trees could grow underneath. The forest here harbours a rich variety of species, both of animals and plants, as compared to temperate woodlands, which are able to sustain much small number of species.

Subtropical forest with broad-leaved trees and dense undergrowth harbour many species of birds, small and large, round the year

There is a great diversity of trees in these forests, but all the individuals of the same species flower together at a marked period of the year. This remarkably wide-spread flowering almost the year round supplies fruits and seeds to a great majority of species of birds at all the times of the year. Even the birds specialized to feed on nectar are able to survive. Many of them take insects in addition to nectar diet. Sub-tropical woodlands are relatively stable, and are reliable source of food for the birds. This is also true of fruit-eating birds such as Green Pigeons, which need plentiful supply of fruits round the year.

These forests harbour a large number of species of birds. Different species have a well-marked breeding period. During non-breeding times, adults set to moulting to replace their worn plumage, and prepare themselves for the next breeding season. Most of the bird activity in such forests goes on in the canopies of trees, where leaves, flowers, fruits and insects are. Birds in these woodlands are generally seen in flocks and mixed parties, probably for the reason that they stand better chances of look-out for potential predators – more watchers are better than one. In addition, some birds are able to find insects disturbed by others.

Birds nesting in these forests face many enemies. So several of smaller species hang their nests from slender tips of branches or from creepers to make predators difficult to reach. They also make domed nests, so that potential predators are not able to see eggs and chicks in them.

Grasslands: Grasslands occur mainly in areas of relatively low rainfall. Climatic conditions in such areas do not favour growth of trees; more so for the reason that extensive fires during the dry summer month may cause serious damage to the plant life. However, grasslands in India are partly the result of burning activities of human population.

Grasslands, which are devoid of trees, are generally poor in birdlife; whereas those with scattered trees have a much wider variety of bird species. Areas, which lie within easy flying distance of water, have many more birds, since most birds need water to supplement their diet.

The most striking group of grassland birds in India include Bustards and Floricans, whose relatively large size with long legs and neck give them the opportunity to spot danger from a distance to make a rapid getaway at top speed. These are good runners, but can fly if they have to.

Many species of smaller birds also inhabit the grasslands; prominent among them are Partridges, Quails, Sandgrouses, Pipits, Larks, Finches etc. These birds live primarily on a diet of seeds, but also feed on insects.

Grasslands with light wooded forest and patches of bushes and scrublands provide habitat to many species of small birds, such as Bushchats, Bee-eaters, Larks, Warblers, Partridges, Quails, etc.

Deserts: Deserts are areas of great heat, but they experience extreme cold at night or in winter. This is because these areas occur far from rain–bearing winds, which modify the climate on land near the sea by bringing warming winds in winter and cooling winds in summer. Rainfall is not only low, but its timing is also unpredictable. Because of the shortage of water, the growth of plant is slow; and if damaged by over-grazing, they may take years to recover.

Some desert areas are devoid of life; but most of these have grasses and small plants. Such places often house a variety of bird species, though these may not be conspicuous. Water conservation in these areas is of overriding importance. As a result, desert birds take what steps they can to avoid unnecessary activities in the heat of the day. They may lie inactive in the shade of bush or a rock or even shelter down burrows, where the changes in temperature are less marked. The closer one is to the sandy surface, the hotter it is. The desert birds have, therefore, evolved relatively long legs. Higher they stand or walk, the less water they will lose. They remain active generally in the early and later parts of the day to avoid heat. Some birds are able to take water from their vegetable diet. However, most desert birds live in close proximity of water. They come to water holes normally both at night and in the morning. Huge flights of Sandgrouses are a common sight making their way to water sources.

Desert birds must shield their eggs and young from the intense heat of the sun. Some smaller birds such as Wheatears nest down burrows or in crevices in rocks. Waders stand over their eggs and young during the heat of the day. Young birds do need water. So parent birds have to bring water to them. Sandgrouses, while drinking, soak their breast feathers in water and bring this water to their young. The Yellow-wattled Plover brings back water on its belly feathers to dampen the eggs to keep them cool.

Some migratory water birds spend the winter months in clear water bodies in dry areas

High altitude birds, such as Lammergeyer, Himalayan Cough, Golden Eagle etc seek their prey in pasture lands adjoining snow line

Mountains: Mountains present considerable challenges to the birds that live there. Oxygen and warmth becomes scarcer with increasing altitude. Above 15000 ft., the air is rarefied and oxygen notably scarcer than at lower altitudes. Temperature drops by 3 F. for each rise of 1000 ft.

The variations in temperature dominate the vegetation. As we go up the mountainside, we may pass from dense lowland forest through coniferous forests to poor, stunted trees, and then to alpine meadows of increasing paucity of vegetation until we reach permanent snow.

In temperate areas, the snowline descends down-wards in winter, and in spring the snow melts away. Birds accordingly spend the winter at lower altitudes than those they spend the summer months. Because of the colder climate and very rigorous conditions, birds that live on high mountains, have shorter breeding seasons. Under such conditions, many small birds roost deep down in the vegetation or down burrows in the grounds.

Many species of birds are restricted to particular habitats on mountains. Because of the habitat restrictions, the birds living there become very sensitive to changes in habitats. As a result, each species exits in very small numbers.

Mountains cause changes in climate. Moisture carried by winds is precipitated as the winds climb up, and as a result, the windward face of the mountain becomes wet and gets covered with lush green vegetation. The other face may get very little rain, and may have much poorer plant life. This accounts for the great diversity of birdlife in mountainous regions.

Alpine meadows are favourite feeding grounds for some ground birds, like Monal, Snow Partridge, etc.

Rivers and Lakes: Life depends on water. So lakes and rivers provide rich habitats to birds. Rivers start as small streams, which join together to form larger and larger bodies of water, until they merge with the sea. The different stages of river provide quite different habitats for the birds. By and large, the upper reaches are steep and fast-flowing. Plants find these difficult to grow in. Hence, food for birds is not always rich at these levels of the river, and birds are scarce, both in species and numbers. Nevertheless, some species are specially adapted for living in such places. The Dipper is a bird of fast-flowing rivers. It forages on the bottom of the streams for small insects.

Downstream, the rivers flow through less mountainous areas with relatively slow speed. Plant life there is much richer, and the birds have more food available to them. Fish-eating birds such as Herons, Kingfishers etc. become more common here. Towards the lower reaches, the rivers become very large and flow more gently. Here one may find an even wider variety of birds, such as Cormorants, Gulls, Terns, etc.

Rivers provide food in the form of fish to many birds, such as Cormorants, Kingfishers, Storks, Egrets, etc.

During the rainy season, the rivers may overflow their banks, and inundate large areas of the surrounding country. The marshlands, thus created, become huge areas of reed beds, and develop into seasonal grasslands. Birds that feed in marshes breed, when the areas are extensively flooded and the growth of vegetation is most marked. On the other hand, birds such as Kingfishers and Herons, that feed in the river, breed when the floodwater recedes, and the fish are confined within small areas of clearer water. It is time for the Kingfishers to make nesting holes in river banks.

Shallow lakes and marshlands abound in birds. Water birds swarm there in large numbers

Seasonal variations also pose problems for the water birds. In arctic regions, waters freeze every year, and the birds have to migrate to warmer areas.

Life in lakes varies in relation to their depth. In deep lakes, where light does not reach the bottom, the plant life can not flourish, and as a result, the whole fauna is very poor. In shallow lakes of less than 20 ft in depth, the plants can get sufficient light to grow freely. Such shallow waters provide very rich habitats of various types.

The shallow lakes and marshlands abound in birds. Cormorants, Herons, Ducks, Grebes, Gulls, Terns, Kingfishers, Coots, Rails, and Waders swarm there in large numbers. Ducks and Rails feed on the vegetation of the lake, but most of the birds take fish. Cormorants and Darters dive and hunt fish under water. Ospreys, Fishing Eagles and Kingfishers dive on them from the air. Herons stalk from the bank. Saline lakes harbour Pelicans and Flamingoes.

Peacock dancing to attract peahens

SOCIAL BEHAVIOUR

Colonial Nesting: Some birds nest in colonies near rich feeding grounds. But most of the species are solitary nesters. Among the fish-eating birds that nest in colonies are the Herons. Heronries often contain a number of different species such as Herons, Egrets, Darters, Spoonbills, Painted Storks, Openbill Storks and fresh water Cormorants. Pelicans and Flamingoes also nest in colonies.

A number of smaller birds that feed on both seeds and insects nest in colonies. Swallows, Swifts and Bee-eaters, that feed on flying insects, are also colonial nesters. Most birds such as Warblers and Tits, which feed on insects collected from trees, are solitary nesters.

Saras cranes dance in courtship display

Breeding Partnership: Most of the birds have monogamous breeding partnership. They form simple pair bonds. Some species are polygamous. Often the male will court a single female, mate with her and accompany her while she builds the nest and lays the eggs. The male then deserts her as she starts to incubate the eggs, and then goes through the same procedure with the next female. In some species, the male takes no part in nest-building, but several of them gather at display sites, where females come for mating. The females then leave, build the nest, incubate and rear the young entirely on their own. Most of the pheasants belong to this group. In a few species, the female lays the eggs and the male incubates and raises the young. In some cases, the female may lay two clutches, leaving the male to raise the first one, while she goes to lay and raise a second. There are exceptional cases, in which male mates with several females who all lay eggs in a nest. The male incubates and raises the young. In few cases, several females lay eggs in a single nest, and then go on to lay 'clutches' for other males to care for. In some species, groups of birds care for the young in single nest. These are called 'cooperative breeders'.

Rose-ringed Parakeets in love

Courtship: Courtship ensures that mating takes place between the birds of the same species. Displays and songs are characteristic of each species, enabling the females to select a correct partner. The prolonged courtship affords chances to a bird to recognize its mistake if it is courting with a member of another species. Such mistakes are likely to occur in species, which are closely related and have very similar plumage. But the species are easily distinguished by their songs, which are different and characteristic of each.

Courtship brings the birds of opposite sex together, increases their confidence in one another, and eventually leads to breeding. Further, continued presence and display of male birds may induce the females to start nest-building. During the courtship process, normally the females remain submissive to the males for most of the period, but in few cases females, such as Weaver birds, are found to be the dominant members of the pair during the height of nesting period.

Courtship involves recognition of the sex of other birds. In many species, the plumages of males and females are very distinct. Ducks and pheasants are a good example; males are brightly coloured and females are duller in appearance. In most species, individuals need to identify the sex.

Courtship leads to pair formation. The most common way, the birds generally follow is that the male occupies a territory, and advertises his presence, mostly through his song. The female approaches, and then follows a prolonged period of courtship during which pair bonds are settled. This takes place irrespective of the fact whether the territory is a large area of woodland or a small colony.

Indian Pied Hornbill offering food to its mate as a courtship gesture

Many birds form pair before they settle down on breeding grounds. In case of birds living in flocks, it is the courting male who closely accompanies the female, and defends a small area around her.

In many species, male displays, and the female approaches him. In some species, birds of both the sexes take equal part in displays. Such displays often involve highly vocal acts, rushing side-by-side, as well as dances in vertical position.

In most species, female lays eggs, and does all the incubation. All this puts a strain on her. She requires more food to form the eggs. During incubation period, she gets little time to collect food. At this time, in many species, the male manages food for the female. Courtship feeding, in some species, is a prelude to copulation. The male brings food items for his mate. In some passerines, male accompanies his mate, while feeding, with pre-copulation song.

Pairs in some species remain together all the year. Geese and Swans remain paired even on migration. Many of the

Doves in courtship posture prior to pair formation

small tropical birds remain within their territories all their lives, and hence stay paired. Others re-pair each breeding season. Courtship seems to be faster amongst previously mated pairs than those that pair for the first time.

The male may undertake a wide variety of displays, including aerial acrobatics and song flights to attract his mate. During these displays, the male shows off the most striking parts of his plumage. The most striking example is the Peacock's train, which is erected into a fan and rustled vigorously in front of his prospective mate. The display of brilliantly coloured birds of paradise is most eye-catching spectacle. Many birds keep their bright colours concealed under their plumage for reasons of camouflage and safety. They show off their bright colours only during courtship displays.

To sum up, the pair formation is not an easy task at first. Birds get to know one another gradually through courtship, and take time to settle down for breeding. The breeding territory is often chosen by the male, and the pair takes quite some time to decide a suitable nest site.

Bank Mynas looking for site for nest-building

BREEDING

Nests: Birds build nests to lay eggs and raise their young. Hence, nest-building is the most important activity, which the birds undertake in their lifetime. A wide variety of predators search diligently for the nests, and make short of them. Some predators are confined to the ground, and many are good climbers and can reach nests in trees. Birds of prey and many members of crow family are serious raiders of the nests of other species. Many mammals including members of cat family, snakes, lizards, ants etc. are responsible for the heavy loss of nests. In face of so many powerful enemies, birds mange to survive successfully. It is a wonder!

There are two main ways in which birds seek to protect their nests. The most widely used one, especially amongst small birds, is concealment. By hiding the nest in an out-of-the-sight place and covering it with camouflaging materials, birds hope to protect their eggs and young. The second method of protection is to build nest in inaccessible places. Birds take great care to visit the nests cautiously so as not to draw attention to it. Predators usually sneak up to the nest in unguarded moments, and take the eggs and chicks. However, concealment by far is the widest method practised to avoid conflict with a potential predator.

Though most of the small birds use both concealment and inaccessibility methods to protect their nests, yet they have almost no defence once they have been located. Many of the small birds suspend their nests from tips of twiggy branches. These nests are also roofed, so that predator may not see whether there is anything worthwhile inside the nest. Nevertheless, life of small birds in breeding season is difficult. However, each time the birds lose their nests, they start again, and lay more than one clutch in a season. Larger birds and the hole-nesters among the smaller species have much higher success in nesting.

Weaverbirds make magnificently woven nests of grass or other stripes of vegetation

Tailor-birds build their nests by folding over and sewing one or two large leaves

A few species make holes smaller so as to reduce the chances of larger birds trying to take them over. Nuthatches plaster the entrance of a hole with mud until they themselves can just squeeze through. In most Hornbills, the female enters the nest chamber, and then the male walls her in with mud until only a small opening is left. He feeds the female through this hole, and she is wholly dependent on him throughout the egg-laying and incubation. After this she breaks out, and the young wall themselves in again, and get fed by both parents.

The nests markedly vary in construction in different species. Some birds such as waders lay their eggs in mere scrapes on the ground. Some birds put only little material into the nest. The hole-nesters such as Owls and Parakeets also put little material into the nest.

The simplest type of nest consists of a flimsy platform of loose sticks in a tree. Pigeons, Doves, Birds of Prey, Herons, Cormorants, Painted Storks etc. build this type of nest. Most of the other species build nests of increasing complexity. However, the most elaborate nests are built by passerines. The Hummingbirds build neatly woven nests held together with spider's web. Some of the Swifts build nests projecting from a cliff face.

The basic passerine nest is built of twigs on a branch of a tree or in the undergrowth. Most of them are lined with grass or rootlets. Many of the Wrens and tropical species build domed nests. Some of the smaller species use lichens, mosses, feathers and similar soft materials in building nests held together with cobwebs. These nests

Swallows build mud-nest against walls

Some hole-nesters drill holes in tree-trunks for building nests (Large Green Barbet)

are extremely warm and well insulated. The most intricate design of this type of nest is reached in some species of Tits. They construct purse-like nests of great intricacy, using moss and lichens bound together with spiders web, and often lined with feathers.

The sunbirds also build intricate domed nests. These are suspended from the tip of a slender branch, so as to be very difficult to reach. The Tailorbirds build their nests folding over and sewing one or two large leaves.

The birds make small holes in the borders of the leaves through which they pass thread of either some plant material or spiders web. Each stitch is made separately, and the ends of the thread are knotted to prevent them slipping through.

Pride of place amongst the avian architects is usually given to the Weaver Birds. They make magnificently woven nests of grass or other strips of vegetation. These are hung from tree, often in colonies. Many are long pendulous structures. The birds enter the nests at the bottom, and climb up through a long tube to the nest chamber at the top.

Herons, Spoonbills, Open-billed Storks, Painted Storks, Egrets, etc. build nests on tree-tops (Grey Heron on its nest)

White-browed Fantail Flycatcher

Eggs: The eggs of birds are hard shelled, often distinctively shaped. The developing chick obtains all its nutrients from within the egg shell. It also obtains the calcium it needs for its bones by withdrawing calcium from the shell.

The size of the eggs varies markedly. The smallest eggs are laid by the Hummingbirds and weigh about 0.5 gm; while the largest, those of Ostrich, weigh about 1.5 kg. If the clutch is large, eggs tend to be small.

The shape of the eggs varies greatly. Eggs of some birds such as Kingfishers and Owls are almost spherical; and those of Woodpeckers and Swifts are long and pointed. The egg surface in some birds as of some Cormorants

Eggs of some Babblers are so glossy that one can see reflections in them (Jungle Babbler)

Eggs of some species are beautifully marked with spots, blotches and streaks (Red-billed Blue Magpie)

is very chalky, whereas it is smooth or highly polished in some. Eggs of some Babblers are so glossy that one can see reflections in them.

The most striking aspect of the eggs is their colour. The eggs of Waders and other ground nesting species are well camouflaged against their background. The ground colour of the eggs of Yellow-wattled Plover differs in different areas, but matches the general colour of the soil within that area. Eggs in dark sites such as nests in burrows or holes in trees tend to be white. In open places, eggs are beautifully marked with spots, blotches and streaks.

Redvented Bulbul

Eggs of ground-nesting birds are well camouflaged against their background (Kaleej Pheasant)

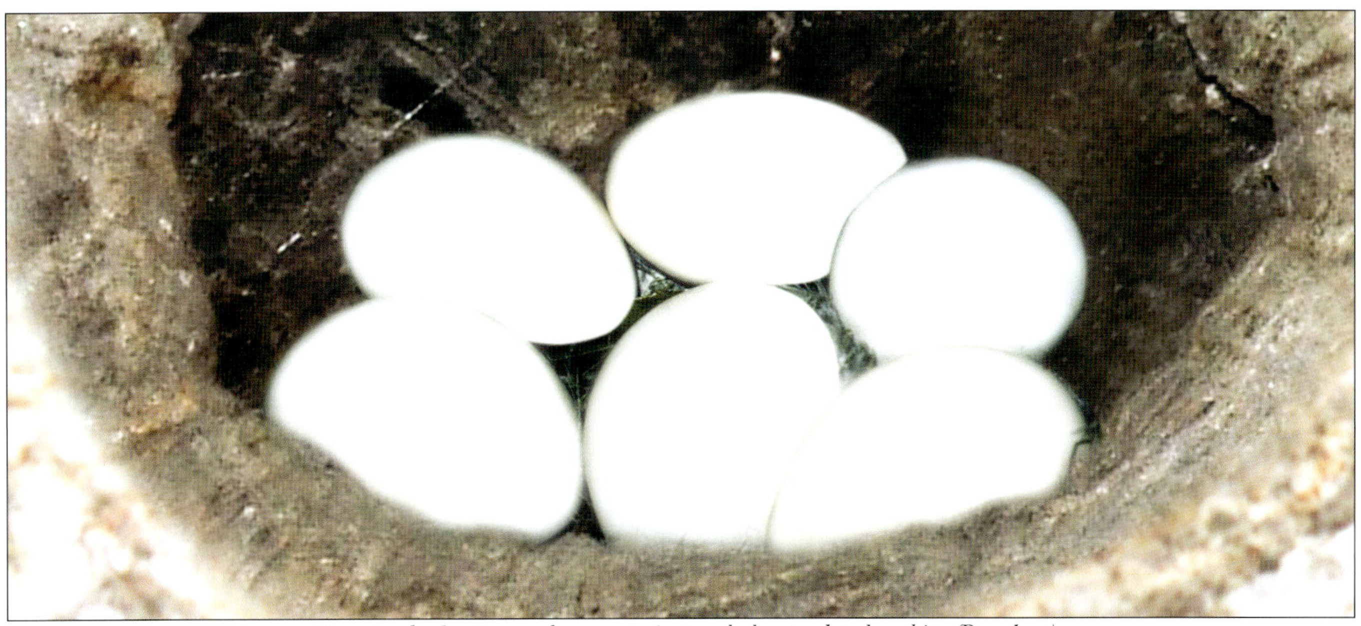

Eggs in dark sites, such as nests in tree holes, tend to be white (Parakeet)

Young of passerines need warmth and protection of their parents during the entire nestling period

Care of the young: Young of passerines when hatch from the eggs are usually blind. They remain entirely dependent on their parents, not only for food but also to keep them warm. In case they do not get this much needed warmth, they may die of cold. These young are nest-dwelling and so remain in the nest for the entire nestling period.

Some birds hatch from the eggs as well-developed and with open eyes. These chicks leave the nest within a few hours of hatching. Even so, these young need parental care and remain dependent on them. These birds are well-feathered and look after themselves from the moment of hatching. Further, they are able to fly within a few hours of hatching. Most of these birds remain in contact with their mother for warmth and protection. Chicks of game birds follow their mother for feeding, and she usually scratches up food for them. In few cases, the parent birds bring food to their young in early nestling period.

Herons and birds of prey usually hatch with their eyes open, but they remain in their nest for the entire nestling period. Owls are also similar, but they are born blind. Young Nightjars are well camouflaged against their background, and though they are able to move away from the nest, which is a bare scrape on the ground, they hardly do so.

The young are vulnerable to predation. The parents have to take great care to conceal their nest from predators. The parent duty demands that the nest must be kept neat and clean. The young produce their droppings packed in gelatinous bags – faecal sacs. The parents eat these when they are small, but as the young grow the sacs become large. Then the parent birds remove them from the nest and drop them at some distance from the nest. In case the nest is in an open site, the parents remove the egg-shell for reasons of safety, as the white material inside the shells may attract crows. Some birds such as crows repeal the attack by administering hard blows with their beak or claws as they pass overhead. Some ground-nesting birds such as Lapwings pretend to be injured and move away from the nest to attract the predators and thus driving them away to a safe distance from the nest.

Young birds need intensive parental care even after they enter the wide world, and start to learn to fend for themselves (Redvented Bulbul with its young)

The chicks of passerines are mostly born naked. The parent bird must brood them in order to give the needed warmth. The amount of brooding that the chicks require primarily depends on weather. If it is colder, more time is needed for brooding.

The food that the broods need varies markedly with the species. Most of the small insectivores bring insect-food, such as caterpillars, to the brood all the day at frequent intervals to ensure rapid growth of the young. Some birds such as Swifts bring back masses of small insects in their throat, after long aerial foraging flights, for their young. Many of the larger birds, such as Herons, Storks, etc. bring larger quantities of fish or other food, which they regurgitate to their young from their crops. Owls and other birds of prey bring large amount of food for their young, but their visits are less frequent.

Sunbird feeding the nestlings

Wire-tailed Swallow feeding its young from the air

Pigeons feed their young with their crop milk – a whitish liquid formed in the crop during nestling period. The young drink it from the crop by putting their heads into the parents' mouths. This method is unique and unusual. Most species feed their young on food, which they normally take for themselves. Some of the Finches are an exception to this rule. They normally feed on seeds, but they keep their young on an insect diet. This is probably because insects have more certain proteins, which the young need for their rapid growth at early stages of life. The young need water. Some birds bring water in their beak for their young. The Sandgrouses have special feathers on their breast, which absorb water. The young sip it from the tips of the feathers.

Blueheaded Rockthrush waiting to feed the nestlings

Parent birds have to ensure that the young may not get injured, while feeding on large prey. Bee-eaters, therefore, remove the stings of wasps before feeding young. Birds, which include snakes in their diet, pull off the heads of snakes before feeding them to their young. Small insectivorous birds usually beat in or remove the head of large caterpillars to ensure that the young is not injured, while the insect is being swallowed.

Birds do make slight changes in the diet during the nestling period. Tits feed small caterpillars to their young, when they are small. This is possibly because these could be swallowed easily. When the young grow large, the parents bring larger prey for them.

Young birds beg from their parents the food they need. When begging increases, the parents go out to search more food, and step up the feeding rates. Small broods, when hungry make noise, and attract predators, and thus, face grave threat to their life. Hence, the parents endeavour to keep the young satisfied by bringing as much food as they can. If the predator is in the vicinity of the nest, the warning cries of the parents silence the calling young. But, sometimes, it is too late.

The number of young in a brood varies widely from species to species. Larger the brood, more the effort is needed to feed the young. Generally, birds do care to see that the brood contains that much number of young which they can successfully raise. Nevertheless, in larger broods, the individuals get less food, and, as a result, for lack of nourishment stand less chances of surviving, as compared to the young in smaller broods.

Apart from the availability of food, life in a brood, to a certain extent, depends on the temperature. The young need warmth, particularly in colder areas. Here they gain by the number. If the brood contains more young; they can get more warmth, which they need, when they huddle together. This is of considerable advantage in cold weather.

The number of young in a brood is fairly characteristic of each species. Ducks, rails and game birds have a large clutch. Whereas waders have smaller broods. With a few exceptions, the small birds, in general, have larger broods than the larger ones. Hole-nesting birds tend to have larger broods then those which nest in exposed sites. Young in hole-nests are relatively safe, and can stay longer in the nest than those of young in open nests.

Birds in many species start incubating only after all the eggs have been laid. As a result, all the young hatch more or less at the same time. In case of species in which the birds start incubating with the first egg, the young hatch one after the other. In this case, the young in a brood are at different stages of their growth. Those hatching earlier tend to be stronger and able to manage more food than their younger brothers and sisters. If, for any reasons, the availability of food becomes scarce in the breeding season, the weaker ones may have less chances of surviving. In case of the young who hatch at a time, all would compete for the food on equal terms, if the food is scarce, all would be weak and light in weight. Birds of prey, Herons, Owls and Swifts belong to this category.

Most of the young need intensive parental care, when they enter the wide world and start to learn to fend for themselves. The parents of most species look after their young during this period. In small passerines, this may be only for a week or so. Others may remain with their parents for much longer periods – say for months – getting limited care from them. Young of some geese may remain with parents throughout southward migration. The young birds so learn the traditional routes and the feeding areas of their parents. Some of the large birds of prey may look after their young for many months after they have left the nest. Nevertheless, the whole process of learning, choosing a territory and breeding are hazardous occupations for young birds, and many perish before they themselves are able to raise their own young.

Nest Parasites: Very few birds have evolved the habit of laying their eggs in the nests of other species. The most prominent amongst them are the birds of Cuckoo family. Koel is a glaring example of this kind; widely known to the people at large. It parasitizes crows. The young of the sexes are black, but when the young have fledged, the females moult into a brown plumage, which they wear for the rest of their lives; though the males remain black.

Cuckoos do not build nest of their own. They leave the whole process of incubation and rearing their young to adults of other species. The latter are called "Foster parents" and Cuckoo "Nest Parasitic".

A female Cuckoo mates with several males, and she may lay as many as twenty eggs in a season. The laying period is usually during May and June. The female Cuckoo keeps watch on host species, when they are at nest building stage. She nearly always waits until the first egg or two are laid by the host before laying her own egg in the nest. She usually removes one of the host's eggs in her bill, as she leaves the nest. The failure to do so means, that she was disturbed, while laying her own egg. Each female Cuckoo keeps watch on one particular species, which is usually an established host, and tries to lay all her eggs in nests build by this species. In many cases, the Cuckoo's eggs bear a remarkable resemblance to that of the host.

Birds of Cuckoo family do not build nests of their own. They leave the whold process of incubation and raising their young to adults of others species (Crow feeding the young of a Koel)

White Pelicans preening their feathers in order to keep them fit for efficient flight

Preening, Moulting and Hygiene

Preening: Birds, which rely on the delicate and intricate structure of the feathers for so many of their activities, need to keep them clean. Dirty feathers stick together and make good hiding places for a wide variety of parasites. The large flight feathers, if pierced or hit, while in flight, barbs separate, and the bird has to repair the feathers at a later stage by preening.

The birds spend a great part of their 'cleaning-up' time on feather maintenance. The bird may bathe in water or in dry dusty earth. This vigorous action helps to shake out foreign objects from the feathers. In preening the bird rubs its bill in the preen gland and distributes the preen oil over the surface of the feathers; particular attention is paid to flight feathers. The action is very rapid, and the preen oil dries quickly. It is presumed that this process improves the condition of feathers. Further, on exposure to ultra-violet light, the oil form Vitamin 'D', which is possibly absorbed through the skin. Some of the birds, such as Pigeons, Parrots and Woodpeckers

Ringdove inspecting its tail feathers to locate area that needs preening

do not have a preen gland. They too keep their feathers in perfect condition. The bird uses its feet as well as its beak to preen the feathers. In some species, pairs of birds preen one another, particularly on the head, where birds cannot preen easily themselves. The bill, however, is mostly used for preening.

Moulting: Though feathers of birds are tough, they do not last forever. A bird has to renew its feathers at least once a year. Shedding old feathers and growing new ones is called moulting. Most birds moult gradually a few feathers at a time, so that they do not have bare patches on their bodies, and do not lose the ability to fly. Moulting usually takes place over several weeks in the late summer, after the breeding season.

Parent birds keep the nest neat and clean by removing the droppings of their young out of the nest (Purple Sunbird)

Moulting is done not only to replace worn plumage, but also to change colours. A special body moult may take place before the breeding season, so that the birds acquire a colourful breeding plumage. The pattern is followed by Divers, Grebes, Plovers, Sandpipers and all other birds, which spend the winter in drab uniforms, and brighten them for the spring and the summer. In some cases, only the male changes so that he will attract a female by his appearance, when breeding time comes.

Hygiene: Birds undertake a number of other hygienic activities, especially in the nesting season. Nesting birds produce their droppings in small gelatinous bags, which can be easily disposed of by the parents. When the young are very small, the parents eat the sacs, but as the young and the sacs get larger, the parents carry them away and drop them some distance from the nest in order not to reveal its site to the predators.

Large Green Barbet removing the droppings of the young out of hole-nest

Migration: Millions of winged creatures move across the surface of the earth each year, and are hardly noticed by most people, as they go about their daily affairs.

Many species of birds regularly fly from one area to another in search of food and shelter, and to escape the rigours of the seasons, particularly the freezing cold of the winter. This is called "migration" and is one of the wonders of the natural world.

Migration is the regular movement to and from a particular area. Most birds travel thousands of kilometers to find better feeding grounds, and more congenial climatic conditions at a particular time of the year. Arctic terns breed around the Arctic circle (near the top of the world) and migrate to Antarctic (at the bottom of the world); thus making a round trip of an astounding journey of 25,000 kms from Arctic to Antarctic and back.

Some get the same advantage by moving downhills. Some small birds breed near fast-flowing rocky rivers and streams in upland and mountainous areas. In winter, they move downhills to feed beside low-land streams and rivers, where there is less cold and more food. This is called "Altitudinal migration".

Since there is enormous altitudinal variation from plains to snow-bound mountains, most of the species of birds are adapted to the seasonal altitudinal migration. With the advent of winter, they move downhills, and with the arrival of spring, they return to upland areas and mountainous forest.

Apart from this altitudinal migration, large flocks of wintering birds, such as Ducks, Geese and Storks, which migrate from distant places in Siberia, Europe, China and Magnolia to the Indian sub-continent, land, on their way to feed and rest in several wet-land areas and shallow water jheels. Several flocks of Cormorants, Ducks, Geese, Storks, etc. have made their home in these shallow water areas.

Life Span: Large sea-birds are capable of reaching the age of fifty, whereas small common birds, such as Tits, Sparrows etc. may survive for their full term of life, i.e., ten years. However, these are lucky ones. The average lifespan of a bird is only about a year and a half even for those birds who survive to become adults.

Demoiselle cranes on migration flight

Red munia

PARADISE FLYCATCHER (Terpsiphone paradisi)

The mature male with its long streamer of a white ribbon-like tail, its silver white body and glossy, blue-black crested head is a bird of arresting beauty. The female has the same blue-black crested head, but its upper plumage are chestnut coloured, and chest and belly are white. The immature male is similar to female. In Sanskrit, this bird is called "*Rajjuvala*", which refers to "ribbon-tailed" because of the ribbon-like tail feature of the mature male. It is practically found throughout the Indian Union, and upto 7000 feet in the Himalayas and peninsular India. It is resident in some localities and migratory in others. It inhabits shady groves, and light deciduous jungle. The agile fairy-like movement of the male, as he flits, twists, turns and darts in the air after insect-prey with its tail-ribbons looping or trailing behind, is a spectacle of astonishing charm and beauty.

It is an arboreal bird with weak legs, but its flight is strong, swift and undulating. Its call is unmelodious and short, repeated at regular intervals. It feeds on flies, gnats and other dipterous insects.

These birds breed from February to July. The nest is a compactly built cup of fine grasses and fibers, plastered outside with cobwebs. The clutch usually consists of three to five pale creamy pink eggs, speckled and blotched with reddish-brown. Both the sexes share parental duties, but female does the major part.

RED-BILLED BLUE MAGPIE (UROCISSA ERYTHRORHYCHA)

The Red-billed Blue Magpie is a common bird in the Himalayan hill forests. Pairs or parties of five to seven are usually seen flying from tree to tree, hunting among the branches of hill oaks, pines and rhododendrons for food. These birds are mainly arboreal, but frequently descend to the ground, where they hop among the fallen leaves with the tail partly cocked, and held well off the ground.

This Magpie is a splendid long tailed blue bird, with black head, neck and breast. Its underparts are whitish, with a conspicuous white patch on nape. The bill and legs are red. An allied species – *Urocissa Flavirostris* – distinguished by a yellow bill instead of red is found side by side over the greater parts of its range.

These birds are noisy, and have a variety of loud, harsh, creaking and chattering calls. They are good mimics, and are often seen imitating to perfection the call of the Pied Crested Cuckoo. Their diet is omnivorous. They normally eat fruits, caterpillars and insects. They seldom miss a chance of joining the miscellaneous mob of birds in the slaughter of winged ants emerging from the ground. The author has seen these birds hoping about near his tent, and picking up kitchen scraps. They are habitual robbers of the eggs and nest-young of small birds. Their flight is slow and undulating – a few wing beats followed by a glide. With the long tail spread, a party of birds in flight makes a charming spectacle.

The nesting season is generally from April to June. The nest is a flimsy shallow, rough cup of twigs, leaves and coarse roots. It is usually built higher in a tree, either on forested slopes or near hill cultivation. The normal clutch consists of four to six eggs, boldly marked with blotches of dark-brown or reddish-brown. Both the sexes are alike, and share parental duties.

YELLOW-BILLED BLUE MAGPIE (CISSA FLAVIROSTRIS)

Yellow-billed Blue Magpie is of the size of a pigeon. It is a splendid purplish blue bird with black head, neck and breast. It has whitish underparts and a white patch on nape. The tail is long and graduated black, and has white-tipped long streamers. The bill is yellow and legs are orange. This Magpie is found throughout the Himalayas from Hazara in Pakistan to Arunachal Pradesh. The closely related Red-billed Blue Magpie (Cissa erythrorhyncha) is commonly seen side by side with the Yellow-billed race in Himachal Pradesh, Garhwal and Kumaon.

It inhabits wet temperate zone with seasonal altitudinal movements from 1000 to 3000 m. Like others of its kind, it is a sociable, and usually seen in parties of five to ten in the company of other species in the same patch of forests. It feeds in open glades, tea gardens, etc. This bird is mainly arboreal but often descends to the ground for feeding. Like their cousin (Red-billed Blue Magpie), these birds are noisy, and are capable of making a variety of loud, harsh, creaking and chattering calls. Though they are omnivorous, but mainly feed on small animals, besides fruits, caterpillars and other insects. They also usually rob the eggs and nestlings of small birds. They produce loud, harsh calls and whistles, and are accomplished mimics of the calls of a variety of other birds.

The nesting season is May-June. The nest consists of a shallow cup of twigs and rootlets near the top of a leafy tree. The bird lays three-four cream-coloured eggs, deeply marked with blotches of dark brown or reddish-brown. Both the sexes share parental duties.

HIMALAYAN TREEPIE (DENDROCITTA FORMOSAE SWINHOE)

The Himalayan Treepie is larger than a Myna, with a long tail of about 12 inches. It is a slender, grey and sooty brown bird with black crown, and elongated central tail feathers, broadly black-tipped. Hind-neck and most of the underparts are ashy. A conspicuous white patch in wing and a small chestnut spot under the root of the tail are its distinguishing marks. Both the sexes are alike.

This bird, as its name suggests, is largely arboreal and inhabits, more or less, thick forest; but sometimes descends into the bushes, and even the ground in search of food between 2000 and 7000 feet elevation in the Himalayan foothills. It has a tendency to accompany other insectivorous birds that rove the hill forests of oak, rhododendron and other broad-leaved trees, and possesses remarkable survival instincts and the skill to adapt itself to the new surroundings. Striated and White-throated Laughing Thrushes are amongst its usual associates. At lower elevations, among the foothills, Sal forest forms a suitable habitat.

These birds wander in pairs or small parties of four or five and keep up a noisy conversation in harsh, rather metallic notes. The flight is undulating, consisting of a few rapid flaps, followed by a short glide. While flying from one treetop to another, they seem to rocket down at a steepish angle on each undulation.

The Himalayan Tree-Pie is an omnivorous bird feeding on fruits, nectar, insects and small animals. It is also a robber of nests and a consumer of helpless nestlings of small birds.

This Tree-Pie breeds throughout the Himalayan range at elevation between two and five thousand feet, and some times upto seven thousand feet. April to July are the most favoured months. The nest is a flimsy platform of thin twigs, coarse roots, tendrils etc. The shallow depression for eggs is lined with finer material. The eggs - three or four – are pale blue or yellowish stone colour, blotched with brown. Both the sexes share parental duties.

STREAKED LAUGHING THRUSH (TRACHALOPTERON LINEATUM)

Of all the feathered tribes of the Himalayan Foothills, the streaked Laughing-Thrush is the most familiar bird of the human habitation between 5000 and 8000 feet elevation. The squeaky whistling songs of these birds are so distinct, clear and mellow that they instantly attract the attention of the passersby. At times, several of these birds seem to challenge each other from different parts of the forested hills, particularly towards evening, when nearly all the other songsters are about to retire to rest. It appears as if each individual is anxious to excel its distant rival.

The Streaked Laughing-Thrush, smaller than a Myna, has olive rufous body, rusty ear-coverts, ashy-grey head, and prominent streaked feathers. Its longish loose tail ends in a black band with terminal grey tips. Both the sexes are alike.

The birds inhabit thickets of wild rose, raspberry, and open hillsides and forests, where there is sufficient low cover. The birds hop in and out of cover, or from branch to branch up a tree, dipping, turning from side to side, and jerking their wings and tail. They largely keep to the ground, and prefer to scuttle away through the bushes on alarm. In the breeding season, the males constantly clamber up to exposed tops of bushes and pour out their peculiar whistling sounds. These birds feed on fruits, seeds, berries and insects, but are often to be seen looking for worms.

The breeding season extends for quite long from March to September. The nest is a deep circular cup of coarse grasses mixed with leaves and lined with rootlets and finer material. It is placed in thick bushes or stunted rhododendron, deodar etc. from four to eight feet above the ground. The eggs – normally three – are unmarked greenish-blue, smooth and rather glossy. The brooding bird slips away quietly only when the visitor reaches within a couple of feet of the nest. It hops about on the ground nearby, and returns the moment the visitor moves away a few feet.

HIMALAYAN WHISTLING THRUSH (MYIOPHONEUS CAERULEUS)

Thrushes form a large and distinctive group in the vast assemblage of birds. Most species are of medium size. The wings vary from short and rounded to longer and pointed, and the tail varies from short to rather long. The legs and feet are rather stout.

Among the many species of Thrushes that are found in India, The Himalayan Whistling Thrush is the most familiar bird. It is blue-black overall with glistening blue wings and tail. It has strong black legs, and stout yellow bill; and looks spotted in good light. Both the sexes are alike. This Thrush is found in the Himalayas from extreme west to extreme east commonly from 6000 to 10000 feet and down to lower elevations in winter. It is a common inhabitant of the hill-streams and torrents. It particularly prefers deep rocky gorges with moss-covered banks overgrown with furs and other vegetation, and with large boulders scattered in wild confusion. In such setting, its sharp and remarkably fine loud song may be heard over the tumult of the waters, as it flies from one part of the stream to another. Its rich whistling song is a delightful performance with a considerable range of notes and variations. The alarm calls, however, consist of harsh rattling and chattering. Thrushes defend exclusive territories by aggressive posturing, fighting and song.

These birds take varied diets, including aquatic insects, snails, spiders, earthworms, molluscs and crabs. Its diet also includes quantities of berries and other fruits, seeds, buds and stems. The birds living near human habitations often adapt to a diet including scraps.

The breeding season is from April to August, and usually two successive broods are raised. The nest is a massive strongly built cup of moss and lichens, mixed with stems, leaves and twigs. The lining is often of finer material, including moss, fur and feathers. The nest is invariably placed on a ledge of rock near or overhanging a mountain stream. Sometimes, it is built on a ledge inside a natural cave or within an occupied outhouse. The eggs are generally three to five, pale clay or pinkish in colour, faintly marked all over with pale reddish freckles, spots and blotches, more numerously at the broad end. Both the sexes take part in building the nest, incubation and raising the young.

ASHY DRONGO (DICRURUS LONGICAUDATUS)

The Grey Drongo is a slender, glossy slaty-black bird, with duller underparts and a deeply-forked tail. It has conspicuous crimson eyes. It is of the size of the common Black Drongo. The sexes are alike.

It breeds in the Himalayas, but descends down to the foothills and farther south into peninsular India in the months of September and October, where it stays until March or April. It is essentially a forest bird, and can be seen perched high up on tree-tops or some such commanding position, from where it can keep a sharp look-out on insect movements. It is strictly arboreal, and can be seen making impressive aerial sallies and swoops after flying insects. From time to time, it pounces on some unwary grasshopper on the ground and carries it off to its perch, where it is battered and swallowed. This bird is a magnificent flier, and hunts until almost dark. It is mainly an insect-eater, but will also feed on lizards, and on the nectar of flowering trees. It produces a number of harsh calls, as well as musical, whistling notes. It can mimic calls of other birds with ease.

The breeding season extends from April to June. The nest is a lightly-built deep saucer of grass and weed stamps, bound with cobwebs etc. It is cradled in a horizontal fork of a branch. It lays three or four eggs, whitish in ground colour with brownish-red spots. Both the sexes take part in all the breeding chores.

Domissele Crane on Migration Flight

PURPLE SUNBIRD (NECTARINIA ASIATICA)

The Purple Sunbird is a tiny, delicate bird of the size of a sparrow. The breeding male is metallic dark blue and purple, and appears all black from a distance. The non-breeding male is pale-olive brown on top, with black wings and tail. A broad blue-black band runs along the middle of its throat and breast, and the lower plumage is yellow. The female bird is olive brown above and a dull yellow below.

This bird has a marked preference for flower-nectar, but also feeds on insects and spiders. Its slender curved bill and tubular tongue are specially suitable for probing into flowers and sucking the nectar. In this process, it helps to cross-pollinate the blossoms. It is found throughout the Indian Union in open lightly wooded country, and is commonly seen in gardens, groves, cultivated fields, scrub country and light deciduous forest. It produces a sharp monosyllabic sound, as it flies about. During the breeding season, the male sings passionately from its favourite perch, frequently raising and lowering its wings, exposing the brilliant yellow and scarlet tufts of feathers.

The nesting season extends from March to May. The nest is oblong pendulous pouch of soft grasses, mixed with rubbish, cobwebs, and adorned with pieces of bark, leaves, twigs, etc. The nest has a portico projecting above the lateral entrance hole, and is suspended from the tip of a branch or creeper at moderate heights, often adjacent to an occupied building. It lays two or three eggs – greenish or greyish white, marked with brown and grey shades. Only the female builds the nest and incubates the eggs, but the male takes part in feeding the young.

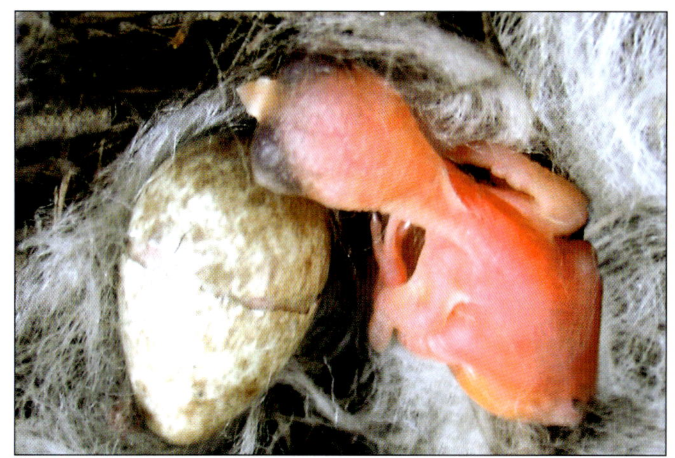
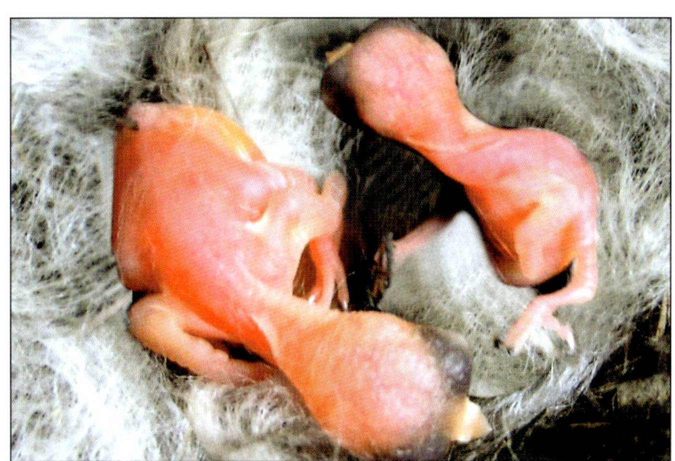

Indian roller

SCALY-BELLIED GREEN WOODPECKER
(PICUS MYRMECOPHONEUS)

This fine woodpecker is about the size of a pigeon – 35 cm. It is dull green above with yellowish rump and scale-like markings on the belly. The male has a crimson crest, while the crest and the top of the head of the female is greyish-black. This bird has a typically long, straight, stout and chisel-shaped bill, and stiff wedge-shaped tail, cross-barred brown and white. Woodpeckers are often heard before being seen. They produce a far-reaching high-pitched sound by rapidly striking the bill on the bark of trees in search of insects. The call is normally of two notes, but sometimes of only one, and occasionally three. They grip the trunk or the branch with sharp claws and press their tails stiffly against the bark to prop themselves up in a succession of jerky spurts. In spring, as a part of courtship, they make a drumming noise by clattering their beaks on a piece of specially selected wood.

The flight of Woodpeckers is strong but markedly dipping, consisting of a few rapid, noisy flaps followed by a short glide.

Woodpeckers inhabit the forests of west-Himalayas, both deciduous and evergreen, including the mixed growth of oak and pine, between 5000 to 10000 ft. elevations, with a little seasonal altitudinal movement. Pairs of these birds are usually seen clinging to the trunks of trees with tails pressed on the bark, working their way upwards directly or in spirals, in a series of jerky spurts.

Woodpecker's chief diet consists of insects lurking in the crevices of the bark, or the hidden pupal galleries of boring beetles. The long wormlike tongue, horned and barbed at the tip, can reach far beyond the bill-tip, and enables the grubs to be extracted from their holes. They also eat ants, and occasionally descend to the ground to pick them up.

Woodpeckers carve out nest holes in large tree trunks from five to 25 ft. above the ground by chiseling away at the wood with their sharp and powerful beaks. The hole consists of a horizontal tunnel, which turns down at right angles and ends in a widened egg chamber.

The breeding season extends from April to June. The normal clutch contains four to six eggs of white colour with broad oval shape. Both the birds share domestic duties.

TAILOR BIRD (ORTHOTOMUS SUTORIUS)

India is bestowed with a wide spectrum of bio-geographic diversity from the Himalayan to the Coastal regions, that harbour a wide range of bird species of the global landscape. The resident species have drawn world-wide attention for their unique behavioural patterns, brilliant colours and amazing habits. One among the many shining stars of the "Birds Galaxy of India", that stands out is the Tailor Bird – universally known for its wonderful skill in constructing its nest by cleverly folding over and ingeniously stitching along edges of one or more large plant leaves, designing it into a funnel-like structure, lined and upholstered with cotton wool, soft fiber from plants and trees and silk thread drawn from cocoons. The techniques employed in the construction of the nest and intelligent variations in the choice of leaves gives the impression that the whole work is the product of skilled and trained craftsman/tailor.

Tailor Bird is a small yellowish-green bird, with a rufous cap on the forehead and whitish underparts. The concealed parts of the tail and wings are pale-brown. It inhabits herbaceous gardens, scrublands, light deciduous forests and shrubbery patches in towns and cities. It is a common resident of the entire Indian Union upto altitudes of about 5000 feet in the Himalayas.

The tailor bird can be seen flitting from branch to branch among the bushes with its tail held erect and flickering from side to side. It produces a high-pitched vibrant call, "towit-towit" or "pretty-pretty-pretty" etc. When alarmed, it rushes aggressively at the intruder with a distinct, "*pit-pit-pit*" call. It is a familiar and confiding bird, equally at home in scrubs, gardens and shrubbery patches of occupied houses, fearlessly hopping and flitting among the potted plants within a few feet of the inmates. It spends its time in gardens where it gleans insects that congregate on the tips of plants. It flies in short spurts which are seldom more than a few meters.

The small bird eats many kinds of tiny insects, moths and butterflies. It also drinks nectar from flowers of Salmalia, Erythrina and other trees. The breeding season usually extends from April to September. Normally, 3 or 4 reddish or bluish white eggs, with brownish-red spots, are laid. Both the parents participate in domestic duties and in the care of the young ones, but the female alone incubates the eggs.

WIRETAILED SWALLOW (HIRUNDO SMITHII)

The beautiful Wiretailed Swallow is about 14 cm. in length, excluding tail-wires. It is glossy steel-blue above, with a bright chestnut cap, and glistening pure white below. Two long fine "wires" projecting from tail distinguish it from its cousin – Common Swallow. Both the sexes are alike, but the tail-wires of the female are shorter.

It is found in the Himalayas upto 6000 feet elevation, and throughout the well-watered hills and plains of peninsular India. Loose parties can be spotted hawking tiny insects over meadows, standing crops, reed-beds or water surface. This bird is highly gregarious in winter. It is a fast and agile flier: a few rapid wing-beats followed by a swooping glide with agile banking and turning movements. Roosts commonly in vast swarms in reed-beds or shrubbery near water. Produces lively chit-chit voice, while chasing winged insects in the sky. The male pours out pleasant musical twittering song in breeding season continuously for several seconds.

The Wiretailed Swallow breeds practically all the year round, but principally from March to September. The food consists of primarily midges, gnats, flies, etc. The nest is a mud-saucer bracket, built out of earth pellets, attached under a culvert or rock overhung near water. The clutch contains three to five white eggs, minutely speckled and spotted with reddish brown. Both the sexes share all domestic duties.

WHITE-EYE (ZOSTEROPS PALPEBROSA)

The White-Eye is a tiny restless olive-green bird – about 10 cm in size, with a greyish-white breast. Its under-tail coverts are yellow, and its chin and throat are a brighter yellow. The conspicuous white ring around the eyes is its distinguishing feature. Both the sexes are alike.

The bird is practically distributed throughout India except desert parts. In the Himalayas, it is found upto 8000 feet elevation, and in peninsular hills upto their tops. It inhabits groves of trees, gardens, orchards and forested areas and woods. It also likes humid evergreen forest.

The White-Eye is entirely arboreal, and hardly descends to the ground. Its pointed, slender and slightly curved bill is especially adapted to reach deep into blossoms to draw nectar; in the process the bird also pollinates the flower. The bird, therefore, is known as a 'flower bird'. It spends its time hunting for food amongst the foliage of lofty trees as well as in bushes, often clinging upside down or sideways like tits to peep into sprigs and buds for insects. Its food consists of tiny insects, spiders, fruits and berries.

White-Eye emits a short nasal-toned call – *'twee-twee-twee'*. Its Sanskrit name '*Saranga*' in all probability, is derived from its call.

The breeding season is practically from April to July. The male bird in this season warbles a pretty little tinkling song from some exposed tree-top. The nest is a cup made of finer grasses, lichen and fibers neatly bound with cobwebs, and slung in the fork of some thin twig at the extremity of an out-hanging branch. It is placed in a bush or tree between three to ten feet from the ground. The normal clutch consists of two or three eggs of pale-blue colour. Both the parents participate in building the nest, incubating and tending the young. Incubation takes ten to eleven days, and the young leave the nest in a like period.

EMERALD DOVE (CHALCOPHAPS INDICA)

Amongst the many species of doves found in India, the Emerald Dove is the most beautiful and colourful of all. It is a brownish – pink dove, with glistening emerald bronze-green upper parts and conspicuous white forehead and eyebrows. In flight, the chestnut underside of wings is its diagnostic feature. In size, it is slightly larger than the Myna: 27 cm. Both sexes are alike. It is one of the widely distributed birds over the entire peninsular India, including Nilgiris and associated hills, eastern Madhya Pradesh and the sub-Himalayan region from Uttaranchal to East Assam up to 6000 feet elevation.

This lonely dove is a dweller of well-wooded country, plains as well as hills. It is particularly fond of foothills, broken up by wooded ravines and clothed with scrub and bamboo jungle. It also occurs in deciduous and evergreen forests. These doves are generally seen singly or in pairs, walking about and picking seeds on dusty forest roads, or in shaded tea and coffee plantations. Their flight is swift, strong and direct; often seen flying across glades at top speed. When disturbed, they fly off with rapid wing-beats at great speed for some distance along the forest path before disappearing into the jungle.

The staple diet of these birds mainly consists of seeds and berries gleaned on the ground. At times, they eat termites also.

The call of this dove is a soft, deep and low *"hoon"* with a nasal ending. It is quite a puzzling sound, when heard for the first time, and takes some time before it can be reconciled and identified.

The nesting season varies according to local and climatic conditions. Since the birds lay more than one clutch in a season, the breeding takes place over a prolonged period. In South India, January and February are the principal months; while in Himalayas March to June are the favoured months. The nest is the usual flimsy twig structure typical of the doves. It is built in a low tree or bamboo clump, five to ten feet from the ground. The eggs – invariably two in number – are creamy white in colour and elliptical in shape.

RUFOUS TURTLE DOVE (STREPTOPELIA ORIENTALIS)

Several species of doves are scattered over the entire Indian sub-continent. These monogarnous, small-billed, seed and fruit-seeking birds are considered to be a symbol of peace and hope.

Long ago, before the invention of the compass, ocean-going merchants used shore-sighting birds, like doves, to direct them towards land. When the ship was on the high seas, and out of the sight of land, these birds were released. They would go to the East, the South, the West and the North, and rise aloft. If on the horizon they caught sight of land, thither would they go.

Amongst the many species of doves found in India, the Rufous Turtle Dove is the most beautiful and graceful of all. It is a large reddish brown dove – about 33 cm in length, with rust-coloured scaly pattern on upper parts and grey-spotted black-and-white 'chessboard' on either side of hind-neck. The tail is round, broad and bluish-grey, with a white terminal bank. Sexes are alike.

This ground-feeding, grainivorous dove is found throughout India upto 12000 ft. in the Himalayas, except the arid portions of Rajasthan and Gujarat. It inhabits in well-wooded country and light mixed forest, and is commonly seen near cities and towns in the Himalayas in summer, where pairs are sighted gleaning on shady paths. When disturbed, they scatter and settle in trees. Its hoarse, mournful "*gur-gur-gurgoo*", repeated in slow runs, is one of the familiar bird sounds heard there. Because doves are preyed on by large raptors, they have evolved several features that allow quick escape. Chased by a raptor with its strong forward vision, the dove's peripheral sight helps keep track of the pursuer, and makes good its escape.

The food consists of paddy, cereals, bamboo and grass seeds. Like other doves, it is a thirsty bird and drinks regularly in the mornings and evenings, and also in the early afternoon.

The nesting season in the Himalayas extends from May to July. In lower elevations, and in peninsular India, it may be found nesting in practically all the seasons of the year, and often raises two or more broods in succession. The nest is the usual flimsy platform of twigs, built in trees or bushes in fairly open forest. The normal clutch invariably consists of two white eggs of oval shape.

SPOTTED DOVE (STREPTOPELIA CHINESIS)

Doves are primarily scrubland birds. Clearing of deciduous forest over vast areas has resulted in the growth of scrublands and dry-lands. The landscapes, thus generated are characteristic of the lands, where water becomes scarce. In this scenario, scrublands form an intermediate zone between dry lands, on the one hand, and woodlands, on the other.

Amongst the many species of doves, the spotted dove is the most widely distributed resident bird over the entire Indian Union, excepting the arid parts of Northwestern region. In size, it is smaller and more slender than a pigeon. Its upperparts are brownish-grey, speckled with pinkish-brown and white spots. The white-and-black markings on the hind neck are diagnostic of this species. The slaty-grey tail with a white border at the end is distinctly visible, when the dove alights with its tail fanned out. Because of its spotted wings, it is called "*Citrapakṣa*" in Sanskrit. Both the sexes are alike.

It inhabits scrublands, cultivated fields and open wooded lands, avoiding arid tracts and heavily wooded areas.

It becomes tame and confiding, and, if undisturbed, freely enters lawns and gardens of the bungalows. Its flight is swift, strong and straight, attained by forceful wing strokes. Like other species of doves, it makes a characteristic aerial display – springing up in the air with wing-clapping, and sailing down in an arc or spiral with outspread tail. It makes an oft-repeated, but somewhat melancholy, long drawn call "*kroo-kruk-krukroo*". It is a grainivorous bird and feeds on grains and seeds picked off the ground or field.

This dove breeds practically all the year round. Its nest is a flimsy structure of twigs, built at a moderate height in a tree or bush. Usually, two pure white eggs are laid. Both the sexes share in all domestic duties, i.e., brooding, feeding and rearing the young.

LITTLE BROWN DOVE (STREPTOPELIA SENEGALENSIS)

In comparison to others of its kind, it is a small and slim dove. It is earthy brown and grey above, pinkish brown and white below with a miniature "Chessboard" in rufous and black on either side of neck. Pairs or loose flocks could be seen in dry scrub or semi-desert areas. This dove is generally found in the drier parts of the entire Gangetic Plain and peninsular India and also in Bangladesh and Pakistan. It inhabits dry stony shrub country in the neighborhood of villages and cultivated fields along with Ring Dove. It is a tame and confiding bird and freely enters in the courtyards of open houses in the outskirts of villages and towns. It feeds on seeds and grain gleaned from the ground. The male bird makes peculiar courtship display on the ground, bobbing and calling, advancing towards a female. It also makes aerial display, rising vertically a few feet on noisily flapping wings and fanned out tail; and then coming down in graceful spiral or arc producing an aggressive prolonged sound *koon-koon-koon.*

The nesting season spreads practically throughout the year. The nest is a usual ridiculously flimsy platform of loose twigs in a clump of trees or shrubs. The clutch consists of two white elliptical eggs. Both sexes share domestic duties.

WHITE-CHEEKED BULBUL (PYCNONOTUS LEUCOGENYS)

Bulbuls are widely distributed family of songbirds, and are found all over India. Of the several species of Bulbuls, the White-cheeked Bulbul is the most cheerful little arboreal bird. It is sprightly earth-brown bird – about 20 cm in length – with black head, short thin superciliary stripe, glistening white cheek patches, sulpher yellow under tail coverts, and white-tipped tail. The crest varies from the rudimentary rounded black tuft of the race occupying Central and Western parts of India to the long forwardly curving pointed crest of the race inhabiting the Himalayan region from 2000 to 9000 feet elevation. Both the sexes are alike.

The White-cheeked Bulbul is found in open scrub jungle and on hillsides dotted with wild raspberry and other bushes. It is tame and confiding, making itself completely at home in orchards and gardens adjoining human settlements. Visitors to the Himalayas are charmed by the abundance and friendliness of these birds near cities and towns situated in the entire Himalayas from west to east. They fearlessly enter the houses and shops for scraps.

The birds usually go about in pairs, but gather in numbers at places, where prospects of feeding are good, such as thickets of ripe berries or swarms of winged ants emerging from the ground. Bulbuls have a number of melodious cheerful rollicking notes in endless combinations, expressing the joy of living.

The food consists of fruits and berries of various kinds, as well as insects, grubs and spiders. While these birds may cause some damage in the orchards or in kitchen gardens, they more than make up for it by the enormous quantities of harmful insects they destroy.

The nesting season is generally from April to June. The nest is a shallow cup of fine rootlets, stems of herbaceous plants and grass blades, lined with finer material. It is placed in a horizontal fork of twigs in a bush or low tree growing in scrub jungle or overgrown clearings. The eggs – normally three in a clutch – are pinkish-white, profusely blotched with brown. Both the sexes share parental duties.

REDVENTED BULBUL (PYCNONOTUS CAFER)

The medieval Persian poets, who have a great sentimental yearning for Nightingales (Bulbuls), conferred the name on this bird, whose cheerful presence throbs most of the Indian gardens with its melodious notes and sprightly disposition. It has a partially crested black head, scale-like markings on the breast and back, and a conspicuous crimson patch on the vent. Its brown tail is tipped with white, and the white patch on the rump is noticeably visible in flight. Both the sexes are alike.

This joyous little bird is found throughout the Indian Union upto 6000 feet elevation. It inhabits lightly-wooded country, scrub jungles and gardens and orchards, both near and away from human habitation. It is a noisy bird and moves about in pairs or small parties. Also they gather in large numbers to feed on banyan and peepal figs and on winged termite swarms. Although arboreal in habit, it will pick food off the ground. The food consists of mainly insects, flower nectar, fruits and berries, and vegetables like peas etc. Though a swift and strong flier, it can't sustain itself in flight for long.

The breeding season extends from February to June, varying with local and climatic conditions. The nest is a cup made of fine rootlets and plant fiber bound on the outside with cobwebs. It is placed in hedges, shrubs, bushes and slender branches of low trees from three to ten feet above the ground. Two or three pinkish-white eggs, profusely blotched with purplish-brown tone, are laid. Both the sexes share in breeding responsibilities.

BLACK BULBUL (MICROSCELIS PSAROIDES)

This bulbul is a slender dark slate-coloured bird with an untidy black crest. The tail is slightly but distinctly forked. The bill and the legs are red. Both the sexes are alike.

It is commonly found throughout the Himalayas between 2000 and 10000 feet, and the hills of Western Ghats and South India. In winter, these birds descend to lower elevations down to foothills. Being arboreal, they are often seen in noisy flocks of six to ten in the foliage canopy of lofty forest trees, flying from tree to tree in company of mixed hunting parties of other birds. The birds affect evergreen forests of broad-leaved trees, and seldom descend to bushes. They often launch short twisting sallies from treetops to capture winged insects in the air. In certain seasons, they gather in large numbers, and the forest resounds with their creaky calls. When chasing one another among the trees, a sharp, long-drawn scream is constantly uttered. These birds also utter a pretty and attractive musical whistle.

The diet of these birds mainly consists of a large variety of fruits and berries. They also feed on insects. These birds are exceedingly fond of the nectar of flowers, such as Rhododendron, Eucalyptus and Erythrina. Noisy flocks, when feeding on these trees, also do a useful service in promoting cross-pollination.

The principal breeding months are April, May and June. The nest is a neat but flimsy – bottomed cup of dead leaves, grasses and fine woody stalks, well plastered on the outside with spider webs, with a lining of fine tendrils and other fibers. It is placed in the fork of a horizontal branch of a tall tree in open forest from 30 to 50 feet above the ground. The clutch consists of two to four eggs, which exhibit a wide range in colouration and markings. The commonest type is white in ground colour, finely and sparsely speckled with reddish-brown and grey. Both the sexes take part in parental duties.

Brahamni Myna

HOOPOE (UPUPA EPOPS)

The Hoopoe, with its striking plumage and splendid crown, has figured in legends, myths and poetic literature since times immemorial. In Ramayana, poet Valmiki symbolizes its call "poova-poova" as a parent's lament for lost sons, "putra-putra". According to Islamic belief, the mark on Hoopoe's crest resembles the Arabic character "Bismillah". Prophet Mohammed, therefore, forbade his people to kill the Hoopoe, because of its moral behaviour. When its mate dies, it does not take a new one, and unlike other birds, it provides care and shelter to its parents.

A Persian legend describes Hoopoe as a friend of Kind Solomon, who gave it a flamboyant crown of plumage. In the 12th century, the Sufi Master, Farid-un-din Attar composed a religious poem "The Conference of Birds", in which the Hoopoe assumed the role of spiritual leader of all the birds in their quest for the wisdom of life.

Hoopoe is of the size of a Myna. Its fawn-coloured plumage is marked by black and white zebra stripes on the back, wings and tail. A conspicuous black-tipped, fan shaped crest extends from its bill to the nape of the neck. Its bill is long, slender, gently curved and sharply pointed. The male and female look alike and are usually seen singly or in pairs. Found practically throughout India, Hoopoe is a resident as well as a locally migrant bird. It inhabits open country adjoining human habitations, lightly wooded forests, cultivated fields, gardens, lawns, scrub jungle and hills upto an altitude of about 7000 feet.

Hoopoe walks gently but also runs rapidly on the ground probing into the soil for food (grubs, worms, pupae, insects and small organisms) with its long pointed bill. While digging, the crest is folded back into a point behind the neck. It is flickered open and erected fan-wise from time to time or when alarmed. It gives a soft but loud call "*hoo-po*" or "*hoo-po-po*", that runs intermittently for about ten minutes, and gives this bird its name "*hoopoe*". Its flight is undulating, and though it normally flies short distances, it is capable of long migrations.

Breeding generally takes place between February and May. The nest is built in a tree-hollow or in a hole in a wall, untidily lined with straw, rags and rubbish. The nest is known for its offensive odour and stench. Both parents perform their parental duties and share in feeding the young ones. It has been noticed that the female is generally reluctant to leave the nest, even when badly disturbed. When the author removed the front slab of the wall to lay open the nest to take pictures of the young, the brooding female pushed herself to the back wall as far as it could and squeezed her body, with her face turned away from the author in utter disgust and fear. Even when fondled with the hands, it remained firmly squatted on the floor of the nest, and did not leave the place. Hoopoe lays 5 to 6 eggs.

MAGPIE ROBIN
(COPSYCHUS SAULARIS)

Robin's fluting tunes are among the most gladsome sounds of nature. Whenever the sun shines warmly over the earth, the males tune their pipe, and enliven the neighbourhood with their melodies. With the advent of the wonderous spring, the blossoms begin to peep forth in every part of the budding woods, and the nature, in all its beauty, promises happiness and abundance to all. Then, it is the Magpie Robin, perched on its favourite fence-stake or the tree-top, lustily gives vent to the warmth of its passion, chiefly early mornings and late afternoons. Its lays are so melodious that they never fail to fill the heart of the listener with pleasing sensations. Everyone knows the Magpie Robin and its song.

During the love-season, the song is emitted with increased emphasis. The male birds zealously guard their breeding territories, and their songs are meant to establish their territorial rights. In Sanskrit, this bird is called "*Srivad Pakshi*" – 'a bird with auspicious voice'. It remains silent during the non-breeding season.

The Magpie Robin is of the size of a Bulbul – about 20 cm. It is a black-and-white bird, with cocked tail. The female is of duller hues, with greyish-blue and brown throat and breast, as against the dark blue-black of the male. This species is widely distributed over the Indian Union, except the arid parts of West-Rajasthan. It inhabits light deciduous forests, scrub jungles, orchards and groves, and likes vicinity of human habitations. It however, avoids dense forests as well as open plains. Its food chiefly consists of insects picked off the ground, and flower nectar as of *Salmalia* and *Erythrina*.

The Magpie Robin normally raises two broods during the breeding season, which extends from March to August. The nest is built in tree holes or in wall crevices. It is made of roots, grasses, plant fibers and feathers. The female builds the nest and broods over the eggs, while the male warns away the predators. Both the sexes feed the nestling.

BLUE-HEADED ROCK THRUSH (MONTICOLA CINCLORHYNCHUS)

There are several species of Thrushes spread over the world, and many of them are wonderful songsters. The common characteristic feature of Thrushes is their spotted plumage.

The Blue-headed Rock Thrush is about the size of a Bulbul: 17 cm. The male is a brilliantly coloured little creature, with a conspicuous white patch on the wings. The crown, shoulders, neck and throat are blue. The rump and underparts are orange-red, and the tail feathers are black, tipped with blue. The female is plain brown above, with barrings and scaly patterns on the underside.

In summer, it inhabits the light forested hillsides of Chir, Pine and Oak in the Himalayas. In winter, it visits practically all India, particularly the stony hillsides covered with light deciduous forest and bamboo jungle, often in the neighbourhood of human settlements and cultivation. It also affects the lightly wooded moist-deciduous areas, but seldom ventures into dense evergreen forests. When disturbed, it flies silently up and sits motionless on an overhanging branch of the nearby tree. From its perch, where it sits bolt upright, it descends to the ground to pickup an insect, and either returns to the perch with the quarry or disposes of it on the spot. Its food chiefly consists of insects, snails and caterpillars, but it also preys on small animals such as frogs and lizards.

In summer, during the breeding season, the male gives out a loud and clear whistling song *'tra-tree-tree'*, heard mainly in mornings and evenings. In winter, the bird remains silent.

This bird breeds throughout the Himalayas between 4000 and 9000 feet elevation from April to July, and often raises two successive broods. The nest is an untidy pad of grass, roots and similar material. It is placed in a hollow in the bank of a steep grass-covered hillside or on a ledge of rock overhung by herbage or under exposed roots of trees. The clutch normally contains four eggs of pinkish-white colour, painted pale reddish-brown. Both the sexes share in building the nest, incubation and tending the young.

KALEEJ PHEASANT (GENNAEUS HAMILTONI)

The Kaleej Pheasant is about the size of the domestic fowl. The male bird is all black above, glossed with steel blue. It has a whitish rump, long white lying down crest, and bare scarlet patch round the eyes. The underparts are brownish-grey, and the tail is long, made of black sickle-shaped pointed feathers. The female is overall reddish-brown with pale scaly markings, brown crest and scarlet eye-patch.

It moves about in small conveys of five or six on precipitous hillsides or ravines covered with tall grass, scrub and oak forest. At the slightest disturbance, it runs head-long downhill. It is interesting to sight this heavy bird, sailing across a ravine on open motionless wings.

The Kaleej is found in the western Himalayas from the foothills up to about 10000 feet elevation. Small family parties come into the open to feed in the mornings and afternoons on forest tracks, and in terraced fields on hillsides. In foothills, they are often found in the company of Red Jungle fowls.

Its food is mainly vegetarian, consisting or shoots, tubers and berries. But it also readily eats insects and small reptiles. The cock makes a loud crow, but, when flushed, it produces a variety of squeaks and chuckles.

The breeding season ranges, according to altitude, from March to June. The nest is usually a crude collection of leaves and rubbish in shallow scrape in the ground under an overhanging rock in a patch of jungle. The normal clutch consists of six to nine eggs, creamy-white to reddish-buff in colour.

BLOSSOM-HEADED PARAKEET
(PSITTACULA CYANDCEMPALA)

The Blossom-headed Parakeet is a slender bird of the size of Myna. The male bird has a bright bluish-red plum-coloured head, maroon shoulder patches and white tips to its long pointed tail feathers. The female has greyer head and a bright yellow collar round the neck. It is resident and local migratory bird throughout the Indian Union upto 7000 feet in the Himalayas. It prefers well-wooded country and forest. Family parties or small flocks are seen in flight, turning and twisting smartly their way through stems of forest trees with astonishing skill and orderliness, uttering their distinctive shrill. The food chiefly consists of wild fruits and berries, but the birds also do some damage to hill orchards. Cones of the chir pine are their favourite food.

The nesting season extends from January to May. The nest is built in a hole in a tree trunk or a branch of tree at some height from the ground. The tunnel is excavated by the birds themselves. Normally these birds do not nest in colonies, but, sometimes, more than one pair occupy holes in the same tree or in other trees in close proximity. The normal clutch contains four to six eggs – pure white, smooth and rounded ovals. Both the sexes share all domestic duties.

GREY-HEADED FLYCATCHER WARBLER
(SEICERUCUS XANTHOSCHISTOS)

This Warbler is a tiny and lively little creature of about 10 cm. in size. It is yellowish-green above and bright yellow below. It has greyish-brown crown, white supercilium and a pale line down centre of crown. The sides of head are greyish-brown. Both the sexes are alike.

This bird is commonly found throughout the Himalayas between 5000 to 10000 feet elevation. In winter, it comes down to foothills and adjacent plains. This species invariably form part of the hunting parties of small birds, that rove about in wooded hillsides, coniferous and open evergreen forests, scrub jungles and gardens, feeding up in the foliage of pine, oak and other trees, occasionally descending into the secondary growth and bushes. It is an active bird hopping among bushes and flitting from branch to branch peering into the leaves for insects, and sometimes catching them in the air. It retains the habits of both tree-warblers and flycatchers, and, as such, derives its name. As it moves about, it emits a distinctive high-pitched call-notes, which the visitors experience as one of the most familiar bird calls. It usually spreads its tail every now and then, and shivers its wings, as it flits about among the foliage. This warbler entirely feeds on small insects.

The usual nesting months are May and June. The nest is built of grass and moss on the outside, and lined inside with wool, fur and feathers. It is always placed in a hollow on the ground, well covered with vegetation, under a bush, or the roots of a tree on a grassy hill-slope, dotted with bushes. The eggs are three or four – pure glossy white in colour and broad oval in shape. It is an interesting and amazing sight, watching a cuckoo (the common parasitizer – the foster parent) feeding the young of the warbler inside the tightly wrapped nest.

LITTLE-PIED FLYCATCHER
(MUSCICAPA WESTERMANNI)

The Little Pied Flycatcher is a small black-and-white bird of the size of a sparrow – almost 10 cm. The male is black above and white below. It has white sides to the base of tail, a large white wing-patch and a broad white supercilium from lores to the nape. Female is olive-brown above with a pale wing-bar and white throat. The upper tail-coverts are bright rufous-brown. It is often confused with several other brown female flycatchers on a casual sighting.

This little bird is a resident of steep hill sides in dense evergreen or deciduous forest, open woodland, orchards, etc in summer. In winter, it migrates to foothills and adjacent plains in secondary growth, especially along streams. It is often seen singly or in small parties in the company of other small insectivorous birds, usually in crown of trees. It utters a thin high-pitched song followed by a low rattling voice. It launches agile twisting and turning aerial sorties after flies all the day and often far late into the dusk, repeatedly returning to its perch after having caught its prey in mid-air. It also gleans insects from foliage or the surface of the ground.

The breeding season extends from April to July. Generally two broods are raised. The nest is a well made cup of dry moss, lined with fiber and roots and hair. It is usually placed in a hole in a tree-trunk in well-forested country. Much of the male bird's energy is taken up in securing a desirable hole and its defence against rivals during the breeding season. When the female arrives in the breeding area, the male tries to lure the female to inspect the nesting cavity through song and parade. During this period, the white areas of the plumage are displayed to their utmost, including the white parts of the tail that are flashed on and off by spreading and closing the tail. The clutch contains three to four eggs, that are usually pale olive-greenish to dull stone-buff with minute freckles of reddish-brown. Some eggs are without markings with considerable variations. Both the sexes share in building the nest and feeding the young.

GREEN-BACKED TIT (PARUS MONTICOLUS)

The Green-backed Tit has white cheeks and glossy black crestless head and breast. A broad central band runs down the middle of abdomen. The back is yellowish green and the underparts are bright yellow. The sexes are alike.

This beautiful and agile bird is found throughout the Himalayas between 4000 and 10000 feet elevation, particularly near human settlements, where it is one of the common and familiar birds. It is an active and bright coloured bird, and is usually seen hunting for insects among the foliage of trees in gardens and orchards, and on hillsides, often quite close to habitations. This joyful and lively bird forms part of the large hunting parties of which the most regular members are the Red-headed Tits, Grey-headed Flycatchers and several species of the warblers.

In the breeding season, the male bird utters a clear, loud and pleasant whistling song, repeated several times. Its food consists of insects, their eggs and larvae, and various berries, as well as fruits and flower buds.

The nesting season is principally from April to June, with a month on either side for early and late breeders. The nest is a heavy pad of fur and wool, built on the thick foundation of moss, grass or feathers. It is placed in holes in tree stumps, hollows in rocks or walls of buildings. A normal clutch consists of four to six eggs – white or pinkish white in colour, speckled and spotted with reddish brown.

GREY TIT (PARUS MAJOR)

This is a sparrow-sized bird with glossy black head and throat. A conspicuous white patch on the cheek is its distinguishing mark. The wings are dark brown with white cross-bars. The tail is blue–black and outer feathers are white. The underparts are white. Sexes alike.

An extremely active and lively bird, the Grey Tit moves about in pairs or small parties on trees in fairly wooded open country. It is a methodical feeder, carefully examining every twig and leaf for caterpillars and other small insects. This agile bird assumes acrobatic positions, hanging upside down and sideways, while clinging to a branch with its strong legs, investigating every square inch of the tree for tasty morsel. The birds spend their time hunting on trees, keeping in touch with one another by means of joyous chirping or twittering notes. They destroy noxious insects, their eggs and larvae, peering under leaves, probing into flowers, and searching lichens and crevices for insects. In addition to caterpillars and other small insects, they eat flowers, fruits, fruit buds, seeds and nuts.

In the breeding season, the male bird utters a loud clear whistling song, while hunting among the foliage with its mate somewhere near at hands. The Sanskrit name – *Syama Valguli* (The Black Song-bird) stands for the bird's sweet voice.

The nest is a soft, shapeless thick pad of fur, hair, wool and feathers, laid on a foundation of grass and moss, with a depression for the eggs, in hollows in tree stumps, or in deserted woodpecker or barbet holes or also in the crevices in the rocks or walls of buildings from five to fifteen feet high. The clutch consists of four to six eggs, with reddish-brown speckles. Both sexes share in building of the nest, incubation of the eggs and care of the young.

Chukar

CRIMSON-BREASTED BARBET OR COPPERSMITH (MEGALAIMA HAEMACEPHALA)

This bird is a small heavy-billed grass-green barbet with yellow throat, crimson breast and forehead, and green-streaked yellowish underparts. It has a short truncated tail, distinctly triangular in flight. Both the sexes are alike.

It is a resident bird of dry and moist-deciduous biotope-light forest, groves of Ficus and other fruiting trees in the vicinity of villages and urban settlements. Like other barbets, this bird is frugivorous, mainly living on fruits and berries. Banyan and Peepal figs constitute its favourite diet. It also occasionally takes insects. This arboreal bird is commonly seen singly or in pairs in parties of a dozen or more fruit-eating birds. This barbet is found in most parts of the Indian Union upto 1000 m. in the Himalayas. In winter, these birds remain silent, but become obstreperous as the breeding season warms up. The call is a loud monotonous *tuk....-tuk....tuk*, repeated every second or two in long runs throughout the day, reminiscent of a distant coppersmith, hammering on his metal. With each *tuk*, the head is bobbed and turned from side to side.

The breeding season extends from January to June. The nest is made in a hole excavated in a dead softwood branch of a tree at a moderate height. If the branch is a horizontal one, the entrance hole is on the underside. The clutch contains three glossless white eggs. Both sexes share all parental duties.

VERDITER FLYCATCHER (MUSCICAPA THALASSINA)

The word 'verditer' ascribes to the green of the Earth. As such, this flycatcher is a conspicuous bright blue-green bird of the size of a sparrow, with a dark patch on the tail and a prominent black mark in front of the eyes. The female is of a duller hue. It is commonly seen in the open forested hillsides and well-wooded areas in the Himalayas from 4000 to 10000 feet elevation during summer. In winter, this bird inhabits, more or less, the entire Indian Union, except the drier portions of Rajasthan and Gujarat.

Perched on exposed twigs or tree-tops, it suddenly darts out and makes agile aerial sallies to hawk winged insects in mid-air in the typical flycatcher manner. Hovering over the spot for a moment, it returns to the same perch, and awaits the next victim. After dusk, it settles down inside the tree canopies for the night. No doubt, verditer flycatcher is a bold and confiding little creature, that freely haunts orchards in the proximity of human settlements. The breeding male constantly sings his pleasant jingling song, similar to that of the White-eye.

Verditer flycatcher breeds in the foothills of the Himalayas. The nesting season is chiefly from March to June. The nest is a thick-sided cup of green moss mixed with fibers and lined with fine moss-roots. It is placed in pockets in earth banks or in hollows in rotten tree stumps or in holes in the walls, fairly low down. The side of a ravine or a steep hillside-cutting for a path are favourite sites. The nest is usually concealed from view by overhanging herbage, but frequently betrayed by the sitting bird darting out in front of the passers-by. The clutch normally consists of four pale creamy-pink eggs, with darker cap-like ring at the broad end. Both sexes share in building the nest, incubating and feeding the young. Incubation generally takes twelve days.

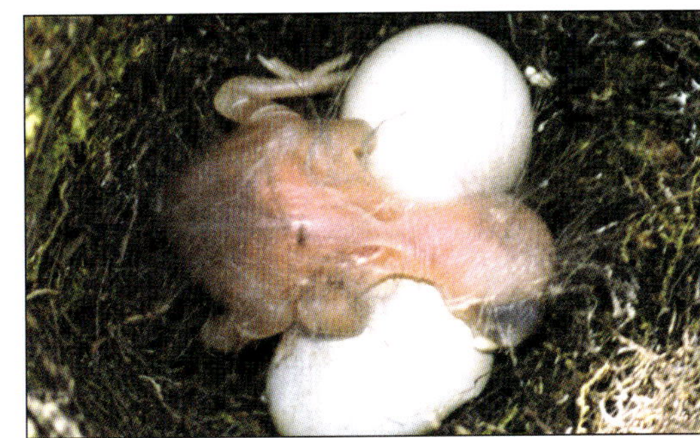

PLUMBEOUS REDSTART (RHYACORNIS FULIGINOSUS)

The male bird is dark slaty-blue with a bright chestnut tail. The female is greyish-brown with white and brown tail.

It is found in the Himalayas from west to east between 4000 and 12000 feet in rocky streams and torrents. In winter, it comes down to lower elevations. The loud shrill call of this pretty little bird could occasionally be heard above the tumult of the waters, while one is walking along the bank of a glacier-fed fast-flowing stream, the waters of which could be seen leaping over stones, dashing against boulders or cascading over the rocky beds. It could be seen flitting from stone to stone or flying from one bank to another in pursuit of food. Each time the bird alights on a stone amid a rocky stream, it opens and closes its tail every now and again or fans it out slowly but deliberately expands it showing a brown triangle broadly bordered with white. From its perch on a stone, it makes short fluttering sallies into the air after winged insects, and occasionally even snatches them up from the surface of the swirling waters. Sometimes, the bird leaps up, catches an insect, and flutters down gracefully on to another stone nearby. All its antics are delightful to watch. The male utters a pleasant but feeble whistling song in breeding season.

The nesting season extends from April to July. The nest is a well-built cup of moss, intermixed with roots and leaves, and lined with fibers, horse-hair, wool, etc. It is placed in hollows in earth banks, crevices in boulders, and under roots of trees alongside streams. The normal clutch contains four eggs – pale-greenish in colour, speckled and blotched with reddish-brown. Both the birds share parental duties.

WHITE-COLLARED BLACKBIRD
(TURDUS ALBOCINCTUS)

Several species of "Blackbirds" and "Thrushes" are common in the Himalayas. They all have a delightfully loud, rich song during the summer months, uttered chiefly in the mornings and evenings. During winter, some of them wander a great deal down into the Himalayan foothills and the plains and hills of peninsular India.

Of the four races of Blackbirds found in India, the White-collared Blackbird is the most elegant and beautiful bird. It is larger than Myna, measuring 27 cm. The male is entirely black with white throat and a broad white collar round neck extending to upper back. Female bird is rufous-brown and paler below, with a dull ashy collar instead of white. Bill, legs and feet are yellow. It is found between 9000 and 12000 feet in the Himalayan oak, Chestnut and rhododendron forests, often mixed with conifers.

Single birds, pairs or small parties are usually met with either on the ground or in trees. But it is mainly terrestrial in its feeding habits, and more commonly seen hopping about, turning over and flicking aside dry leaves in search of insects, and ripe wind-fallen fruits and berries.

It breeds in summer in the Himalayas, and during this period, the male bird utters a loud, rich, melodious song with a fine range of notes. Its melody is invariably interlinked with the calls of a large variety of other birds, all perfectly reproduced. The forest resounds with the chorus of full-throated songs from every direction, as each bird tries to outdo its neighbour. The rivalry does not end with the music alone; for the males become extremely quarrelsome at this season.

In winter, the birds are shy and mostly remain silent. The flight is swift and direct without pauses in wing-beats or gliding.

Its diet consists of insects, grubs, fruits and berries. It is also found of flower nectar.

The nesting season ranges from May to August. The nest is a deep cup of moss, rootlets and grass, lined with soft fern and root hairs, usually built in trees about 15 feet from the ground. It lays three to five eggs; pale-white blotched with dull-brown, rather densely at broad end. Both the birds share parental duties.

Yellow-legged Green Pigeon

SPOTTED MUNIA (LONCHURA PUNCTULATA)

The Spotted Munia is of the size of a sparrow – about 10 cm. It is dull chocolate brown above with yellow and lighter brown bars; the sides of head, neck, chin and throat are chestnut. Breast and flanks are speckled black-and-white. The upper tail-coverts are golden fulvous and the belly is white. The rump is barred with white. Sexes are alike.

These birds are found throughout the Indian Union, excluding the arid zones of Rajasthan and Punjab, upto 7000 feet in the Himalayas in open country, grassland, gardens and cultivation. Like other Munias, the spotted Munias are basically seed-eaters, and consequently equipped with thick bill. These are usually seen hopping about and gleaning grass seeds on the ground in large parties. When disturbed, these birds fly away in close formation into the tree and bushes, uttering a faint but sharp twittering "*tee-tee-tee*". These birds roost huddled together, sometimes with weavers and other Munias.

Munias are ground-feeders, as such, they eat small seeds, ants, beetles and variety of small insects picked off the ground. They also occasionally devour winged termites emerging from the ground.

The breeding season is mainly from July to October. The bird builds a large globular nest with the help of various sorts of grasses. A circular entrance, only sufficiently wide for the bird to enter and leave with ease, leads on to the egg-chamber, lined with finer grasses and vegetable fibers. The nest is usually built in a thorny bush, six to ten feet about the ground. A normal clutch consists of four to eight pure white eggs. Both the sexes perform all the domestic duties.

Saras Crane

JUNGLE BABBLER (TURDOIDES STRIATUS)

An earthy brown and untidy looking bird with a longish tail, which gives the impression of being loosely stuck into body. Both the sexes are alike. These birds are invariably seen in flocks of half a dozen or more. Hence, they are popularly called "*Sat Bhai*" in Hindi and "*Seven Sisters*" in English. They are found throughout the Indian Union, Bangladesh and Pakistan, both in plains and hills upto 2000m elevation. They constitute six races, mainly on differences in colouration. These birds inhabit outlying jungles, well-wooded compounds, gardens and groves of trees near towns and villages. Flocks of these birds are commonly seen hopping about on the ground, making thorough search amongst the fallen leaves and twigs for moths and other insects. They generally form the nucleus of the mixed hunting parties of birds in forests. The birds usually keep up a constant conversational chatter and squeaking. This occasionally develops into a loud noisy wrangling. They remain sociable even while they are in the process of making pairs and building nests during the breeding season. They feed in flocks and band together to ward off attack by predatory hawks and cats. Their food consists of spiders, cockroaches, and other insects and larvae. They also eat wild figs, berries, grain and nectar of flowers, coral, silk cotton and other trees. They breed irregularly throughout the year. The nest consists of a loosely built cup of twigs, rootlets and grass in the fork of a leafy branch. A bird lays three or four turquoise blue eggs. Parental duties are shared by both the sexes or even communally. Sometimes, two birds lay their eggs in one common nest.

Fishing Owl

WARBLERS

Warblers are small birds with slender bills, specialized for gleaning insects from leaves, grasses and twigs. Because most of warblers look alike, the several different species are not given individual names in Sanskrit, and are referred as '*Chatika*' – 'little bird' and '*Patingika*' 'little sparrow'.

Warblers make up a huge family of several species, most of which are scattered throughout the Indian Union, both in deciduous and moist deciduous areas, including reed beds. A few species inhabit at higher altitudes upto 10000 feet in the Himalayas. Most of the species of these birds have drab brown and grey plumage. In the main, these are insectivorous and feed chiefly on insects: caterpillars, ants, small beetles etc.

The warblers, as their name indicates, are renowned for the quality of their songs. These birds utter in gentle continuous trilling manner. It appears as if they speak in verse or give expression to their passions in songs. They keep singly or in pairs or in small parties in scrub jungles, gardens and orchards. These tiny birds are mostly seen flitting jerkily from bush to bush with constant flicking of the tail.

In breeding season, the males give a spirited performance from an exposed perch excitedly warbling their squeaky songs. The breeding takes place over a prolonged period from March to September. Different species build different types of nests, depending on the vegetation growth and the climatic conditions of their respective habitats. Reed warblers construct a deep massive cup of dry reed leaves slung between several reed stems above water. The nests of scrubland birds are a rough cup of twigs, grass, roots and stems, lined with fine grass, wool, hair and fibers, well hidden in low thorn bushes or clump of grass. Some species build a rough dome or oval pouch of grass, moss etc. close to the ground, while a few make a ball of moss, lichen and dead leaves, and place it among the roots of trees or hollow tree trunks.

These small birds lay several eggs ranging from three to ten. The eggs are glossy and of oval shape, and in most cases profusely blotched with brown. Both the sexes take part in the performance of parental duties.

A PAGE FROM THE BOOK OF NATURE

The Book of Nature has endless pages. It has no beginning, and there is no end to it. One can open any page, and start reading it. A White-eye reads one of the pages.

We built this house towards the end of March on the leafy branch of a citrus tree in the midst of a well-wooded forest on a mountain slope facing the snow-clad Himalayas. We used the finest quality material available in the surrounding area. We designed it in a bowl shape, so that our children could breathe fresh air, and, sitting comfortably in it, could look around and enjoy the scenic beauty of the pristine wilderness of this mountain land.

I laid two eggs in early April. The babies would grow young in three weeks, and would have, by then, strong wings to fly to safer places before the onslaught of rains and hailstorms that might lash this region in May or June. If rains are delayed, forest fire would pose even greater threat both to our house and children during the dry summer months.

The babies are hardly a week old. They are tender, and need careful protection both from the heat of the hot hours of the day and the evil eyes of predators. So we keep them under the umbrella of our bodies to ensure their safety.

While I stay with the babies, my husband goes out to procure food for them. The moment he returns, I go out in search of food, and he takes my place. We perform our duties by turn.

The babies are growing every day. They need healthy food. We procure the best quality fresh food available in the surroundings of our house. See, the variety of food we provide to our babies.

For a balanced and healthy growth, the babies need extra dose of calcium. We feed them small bits of egg shells from which they had sprouted out. We, too, require calcium, for we get exhausted in performing our parental duties from dawn to dusk. So we also take bits of shells.

The babies are growing fast. They have put on feathers and have opened eyes.

We always keep our house neat and clean. Our babies are small, and can not go out to answer the calls of nature. We take out regularly the droppings of our babies to provide a healthy environment.

Our babies have grown young. They are now strong enough to lead a free and independent life. One is sitting comfortably on a leafy perch near the house. The other one is seated confidently a little far, unmindful of any danger that might be lurking him. Probably, they are eager to explore the world around them in which they have to live and spend the rest of their life. See, how pretty they look in flight. Soon they will be out of our sight. Alas! We will never see them again. The house now looks empty and deserted. We worked hard for days together to build it, braving chilly winds and scorching heat. Prior to their birth, we used to live freely in the garden of Nature. We had never felt the need of a house. This is what the Nature has ordained for us. However, we have performed our parental duties. Let us also leave this place, so that the loving memories of our dear children may not trouble us for long. Thus, with heavy hearts, we took a long and nonstop flight over the vast mountains, till the setting sun warned us of the approaching darkness.

The empty and deserted house still stands as a monument to the happy family life that once we lived here.